CHOOSE
YOURSELF

*A Journey Toward
Personal Fulfillment for Women*

DR. NICOLE LaBEACH

VOLITION ENTERPRISES, INC.

For information, contact:

Volition Enterprises Inc.
5482 Wilshire Blvd.
Los Angeles, CA 90036.

This publication is published with the understanding that the publisher and author are not engaged in rendering psychological services (e.g., counseling or psychotherapy). If legal advice or professional psychological advice is required, the services of a competent licensed professional should be sought. Additionally, any similarities between the subjects in this book and any individual is coincidental.

To place an order visit our Web site at: www.volitionenterprises.com

E-mail us at: yourvolition@aol.com

Published by Volition Enterprises. Los Angeles. Atlanta.

Design and Typesetting: Launi Wilson-Medley and Jason Medley
Editing: Chandra Sparks Taylor
Back Cover Text: Crysta Bragg, Emilia Serrano, and Nicole LaBeach
Logo Designer: Christopher Pike

Library of Congress Control Number: 2002096264

First Paperback Edition

ISBN 0-9726634-0-1

Dedication

In Heaven:

I would like to dedicate this book to my Lord and Savior Jesus Christ
You were so I could be. May the words of my mouth and the
meditations of my heart forever be acceptable in thy sight.
To Carlos and Grandma Alice, you will forever be missed.

On Earth:

I would like to dedicate this work to my mother, You are and will
forever be my gift from God. Thank you for everything. No words
can express my love, admiration, respect, and gratitude.

Acknowledgements

*O*ne morning I was driving and before I could park at my destination the vision of this book was revealed. From that day forward, I embraced the journey of writing and all that it entailed. With a blank computer screen, thoughts moved from my mind to what you now hold in your hands. One mocha frappuccino after another I turned Starbucks into my second home and my laptop into my best friend. From that day to now, this process has continuously blessed me. As I moved from one chapter to the next I had a lot of help along the way. To Mommy, I love you and dedicate this book to you. To Calvin, the love of my life, thank you for being my supporter, my God-sent love, and friend. Words are indeed powerful, I wrote *Could It Be* and then you came bringing life to my words. You are the editor I could have never imagined. May we continue to love each other and praise Him for the rest of our lives. To Andrea, I thank you from the bottom of my heart. You were definitely a blessing to me in my efforts. I can't wait for your words to be published. The world is not ready for *The Necklace* but they will be. You are a dynamic woman, and I have learned a lot from you. To Dad, thank you for supporting this project and being a better man. Your efforts toward a better us is a blessing. To all of my aunts (you know who you are), thank you for being motivators, never- ending supporters, and towers of strength from which I could learn. To my uncles (you also know who you are), thanks for all your help and wisdom. To my cousins, I am blessed that we are related. No matter the distance, each of you are but a phone call away (what more could a girl need, want, or ask for?). To my friends, thank you for not telling me that I was crazy for trying to live up to my purpose. Our conversations and times of laughter helped me complete this part of my travels. For all the talks and laughs, I thank you. A girl is truly blessed when she has women and men like you to call friends. To the women that traveled from near and far on those special Saturdays to share their thoughts, a million thanks will never be enough. Your thoughts made this project more real, and your time will forever be considered a gift. To my unofficial editors, thank you for reading draft after draft. Your comments "kept it real." To Dr. Harvey, thank you for educating me and continuing to be the Big D. To all the other people who helped me along the way, your kindness, support, and inspiration will never be forgotten. Travis Hunter, thanks for taking the time to help a new author learn the ropes. Chandra Sparks Taylor, your editing expertise was truly appreciated. To my godbrother Michael, thanks for your love, editing, belief in my voice, and marketing savvy. Lisa Hoggs, thank you for promoting this book for women to receive and embrace it all over the world. Launi and Jason, thanks for your artistic abilities and expertise. To Crysta and Emilia, your written words were well received, thanks for all of your help. To my investors, each of you were angels of delivery. Your belief in me made touching the lives of many a possibility. To anyone I have not mentioned, please charge it to my mind and never my heart.

Many Blessings,
Nicole

TABLE OF CONTENTS

Foreword

Throughout time, society has promoted the notion that men have the right to choose. This concept has been nurtured in them as their birthright. In this vein, it often appears that men are encouraged to engage in activities that promote personal evolvement, fulfillment, and self-preservation. Women, on the other hand, are often required to fight for their right to choose and frequently learn to engage in behaviors that are more self-destructive than self-promoting. In fact, many of us have defined our womanhood by the ability to place our personal needs, aspirations, and potential behind that of others. As a result, the diligence with which many of us care for ourselves is often minimal. It's simple but yet so complex: As women, we must begin to acknowledge, own, and embrace the right to choose ourselves. This is not a women-against-men philosophy, it's a woman, love, regard, and heal thyself emergency!

From childhood to adulthood, we all experience threats to our sense of self and self-worth. As women, many of us desire respect, opportunity, and equality for ourselves and our gender. However, what we struggle with the most is the attainment of true personal fulfillment—the ability to feel good from the inside. The intense stress, suppressed anger, and unresolved issues that plague our everyday lives often make internal happiness seem impossible to achieve. As we try to seek shortcuts (e.g., material things outside of ourselves) to contentment, many of us have recognized there are none. Some of us can even admit that true internal happiness is not derived from things outside of ourselves. Of course we all experience moments of joy, but true happiness stems from a strong sense of inner peace. It manifests from a love, acceptance, and nurturing of self. In fact, fulfillment is probably the one thing we have the most control over because it starts with our power to choose, change, and forgive. With one life, one spirit, one body, and one mind, we cannot afford to continue doubting this truth.

For many of us, the desire to live a fulfilled life is a consistent one. However, achieving this desire requires a skill that most of us have yet to master, the ability to choose ourselves (e.g., stop beating up on ourselves, stop putting everyone else's needs before our own, and start living a life that embraces personal purpose). In its essence, it's an exercise in caring for your best and most important asset—you.

As a woman, I, too, have been on the relentless search for true fulfillment. It took a lot of tears, honesty, and soul searching to recognize that a fundamental aspect of my inability to achieve a consistent sense of personal contentment stemmed from my inability to choose myself. I smiled a lot and acquired one status symbol after another, but nothing changed the fact that I often felt like I was living a life I didn't want. As I moved through life's accomplishments and challenges, I questioned feelings of emptiness and guilt for seeming unappreciative for the life I had. One question after another, the answers were often the same: If I had..., If he hadn't..., If I could..., If I did..., If she would have..., I would be... All of these were answers to explain why I felt unfulfilled. One excuse after another, I attempted to fix the surface yet wondered why my efforts always failed to reach my heart. I tried almost everything but nothing worked for very long. I needed to do something, but I wasn't sure what. So, with hesitation, I dared to do something new. I tried working on myself from the inside out. As I began my journey, I recognized that I had to start learning how to choose myself—a new approach to my womanhood. I could no longer live life based on the expectations, choices, and opinions of others. For the first time I had to be brutally honest about who I was, how I felt, and what motivated my actions and behaviors. In essence, I had to acknowledge and release my emotional baggage and take responsibility for my life. As my healthier self emerged, I discovered what I wanted, embraced who I was, and chose to start living.

Difficult as it may be for some of us to admit, personal contentment is chosen, not given. As women, no one is responsible for our happiness except us. It's up to us to develop a sense of authority over the past, appreciation for the present, and boldness for our journey toward the future. No longer can we continue to do the same thing and expect a different result. It's a new day, one that is ours for the choosing.

It is my hope that this book will help to make your path toward fulfillment a bit easier to travel. May the chapters be a thought-provoking ride that moves you from past pain to a more realized sense of potential, purpose, and prosperity. As a vehicle of self-discovery, be ready to think about where you are, how you got there, and where you want to go. The poetry, chapters, and Insight Corners will challenge you to move within a journey of emotional empowerment. Part I, the journey *From There...* employs an understanding of what may be holding you back from personal fulfillment and Part II, the journey *To There...* explores tools to create and choose the fulfilled existence you desire. Each chapter begins with a poem that prepares you for the text and ends with questions that will serve to customize your own journey. These questions are part of what is called the Insight Corner.

The Insight Corner promotes further dissection of the chapter content to present additional opportunities for personal discovery. Answering these questions will jump-start your movement from there...to there...by promoting reflection, awareness, and change. At times the road to choosing yourself will seem bumpy, but I challenge you to take the trip. It promises to be one of the best you've ever taken—the journey toward a more evolved self. With that, may the destinations of understanding, love, and clarity be true havens you never choose to leave!

THE SHELTER

Simply put

Is it worth it
To lose the self you've found?

You've crawled through glass to find you
Now you feel the mirror is pulled
Because he just keeps on spewing
That you just ain't no good

Well
If no good is true
Why is he still with you?

Could it be that you complete him?
Giving his life meaning

Bearer of fruits
Nurturer of roots
Yet he claims you have no meaning?

Your name is Woman
You bring light through life
Wisdom through words
And comfort through your center

You are powerful beyond measure

Don't be fooled by his anger or words that intend to destroy
He's just a little jealous
That your spirit represents joy

Please dare to see
A real man will respect you

He'll love you in all your splendor
He'll know deep within
That manhood is only found in loving who he is
In spaces free to see
That you are the half that makes him whole
The Mother
The Lover
The Bearer of His Soul

Introduction

rue living requires we embrace life as time that is filled with endless possibilities. However, it is very difficult to see the "possibilities" and recognize your "worth" when you are surrounded by darkness. Picture a glass filled with water. If the content is purified, one can easily see through it. This exercise becomes a bit more difficult if the content harbors debris or what I contend are colors that promote an obstructed view. In taking a closer look at this example as though it were a metaphor of our emotional well-being, I wish that you would pose two sometimes painful questions: What color is my water? And, what have I allowed to obstruct my view, path, and outlook?

In general, we are born with a metaphorically clear glass of water. Our formative and adolescent years promote the intake of vast amounts of information that alter the content within our glass. We innocently receive metaphoric debris or colors with a lack of mastery for discerning good particles from bad. With untrained filters, we encounter experiences and digest information with an inability to protect ourselves from their effects. This process is continually perpetuated throughout our youth. Ironically, many of us still endure this process as adults. As in our younger years, many of us have yet to master the filtering and maintenance processes of life, which allows us to discern what should be collected and purged as it relates to our glass. As children, we were not responsible for what tainted our water. Living in a less-than-perfect family, environment, and society, we all entered adulthood with varying amounts of debris. However, as we take strides toward a greater sense of purpose, wholeness, and fulfillment, we cannot ignore the need for a functional purification system. As we learn to choose ourselves, the value of purified versus debris-filled water becomes critical.

For all intents and purposes, the foundation of our personal outlook, esteem, and efficacy is based on the makeup of our metaphoric water. Thus, we must all strive for it to be purified and clear. In adulthood, this clarity is often determined by the ability to: 1) remove destructive colors from our glass, 2) protect our glass from the introduction of negative colors/debris, 3) ward off continuous recontamination, and 4) implement behaviors that maintain purified content. This clarity promotes insight, opportunity, and purpose. However, the lack there of perpetuates fear, dysfunction, and turmoil. The importance of this water-coloring concept occurred to me when I volunteered as a support-group counselor at a battered women's shelter. My time there reinforced the critical need for every woman to audit the colors of her past and their manifestation in her present. The experience forced me to recognize that each of us owe it to ourselves to be more active than passive at debilitating and removing debris to maintain content that promotes personal value, growth, and happiness. In hindsight, my work with these women started me on a journey of personal discovery from there... (my own past) to there... (a sense of peace and personal fulfillment).

While at the shelter, I connected with many of the women, but one forced me to see the reality that choosing ourselves is truly a foreign concept to many of us. She was a nurturer, helper, and caregiver in her profession. However, she, too, was a victim. Beneath her work uniform were countless bruises (old and new) spanning more than thirty years of abuse. Her bruises stemmed from years of physical and emotional water coloring that promoted a sense of powerlessness in her situation. Perpetuated over time, the colors she received made her an expert at decisions that promoted physically and emotionally destructive outcomes. Back then, it amazed me to hear her speak. My youth and inexperience often made it difficult to believe anyone could be subjected to the mutilation she endured from childhood through marriage. Time and circumstance had colored her water and left her with debris she never learned to filter. As a result, she saw herself as worthless and worthy of one abusive situation after another. The colors she experienced distorted her view and made it impossible for her to realize, embrace, and own her possibilities.

As I became familiar with her, I recognized her personal façade (e.g., an empowering profession) evidenced the similarity between tap water (clear but not lacking impurities) and purified water (clear and devoid of impurities). As a caregiver in the community, she had covered the impurities of her content well. Her high level of functioning within her job almost made it easier for her to avoid the impurities in her glass and render the debris undetectable to others. Though she sought to empower and be supportive to others, she often felt helpless and powerless. Childhood sexual abuse and two generations of domestic violence defined the heaviness of her emotional baggage and tried to irretrievably break her spirit. Her decision to seek help from the shelter would be one of her first attempts to unlearn what she had been taught, take back her life from both the inside and out, and learn to choose herself. To do so, she would have to release the debris that plagued her adulthood with denial, victimization, and low esteem. Through therapy, she engaged in the ultimate fight of her life: to move beyond survival toward a sense of empowerment and freedom.

Though some of you may view her situation to be extreme and shy away from how her experience could possibly resemble your own, I pose the question again, what color is your water? As many of us suffer in silence, we endure unfulfilling relationships, carry destructive emotional baggage, and minimize the need to care for and love ourselves. No, many of us have not endured the extreme treatment this woman did, but on a voluntary basis we embrace too many situations that hinder personal growth and fulfillment. With colored water and an inability to purify it, many of us have struggled to peek through darkness and grasp rays of light. We seem to fit one of three scenarios: 1) a woman whose filters are virtually inactive because she takes and keeps any debris she receives; 2) a woman whose filtering systems are intensely overworked because she frequently purifies her content but keeps allowing the same unhealthy particles into her glass time and time again; or 3) a woman who is learning to master or has mastered the art of removing debris and maintaining clarity. Which woman are you?

If you are in the first or second group, it's time to take a serious look at the impurities that reside in your glass and ponder the question: Would any sane person drink this? As we forever pride ourselves on mastering the Art of Others, too many of us have diminished the need to master the Art of Ourselves. Think of it in terms of a newborn child and mother relationship. What would the level of debris in your water be if you monitored your glass like a mother watching what is ingested by her newborn? As women, it's time to take this same care for ourselves. True empowerment will only come when we adopt a willingness to choose ourselves by loving, nurturing, and protecting ourselves. It requires that we clearly dissect where we are, how we got there, and where we want to go. This exercise enables us to identify and label the undesirable colors that need deactivation and removal. Therefore, if you recognize verbal abuse as one of your contaminating colors, it's up to you to filter this color and make a conscious decision to discontinue engaging in behaviors and situations that reinforce it. Only you can make choices that filter and protect you from the destructive effects of this color.

Once you've filtered the contamination, the maintenance process must begin. In keeping with this example, restraint from situations that represented verbal degradation would be necessary. Much like a recovered alcoholic, taking one teaspoon of vodka after being sober cannot be safely explored. Why? The history of alcoholism makes even a teaspoon of alcohol harmful. Therefore, knowing that verbal abuse is a symbolic color of your past, part of your maintenance process would entail abstinence from communicating with people who are unable to control their anger (violent communicators) or those who believe they have the right to relate to others in any inappropriate manner they choose. In this scenario, anything short of this process would threaten your goal of sustained clarity.

As you will see throughout this book, all of us have the right to protect our water from toxicity. If we don't, we carelessly feed into situations that move us farther away from the health, clarity, and fulfillment we deserve. As women, we have become so used to receiving accolades for taking care of "him," "it," and "them" that we often ignore the need to take care of "us." As a result, personal needs are often dealt with on a reactive rather than proactive basis, and the promotion of "you" gets lost. The following chapters invite you to redirect and eliminate unhealthy behavioral patterns, resolve dysfunctional relationships, take dominion over past events, and lose deadweight. This wouldn't be the worst thing you've ever done. Then it moves you beyond the past and propels you toward an appreciation for life and the discovery of personal purpose. As you embark on this journey of personal discovery, be prepared to gain strength, insight, and encouragement. As you move from chapter to chapter, you will engage in a filtering process that's all your own.

Now, the question is, will you take the process seriously and filter your content until you can see clearly? As the author of this book, I can only hope that you will value your journey and be open to clarifying your content as you go. The truth is, no matter your circumstance, your life has a purpose. However, this truth is often shadowed by obstacles, pain, and fear. It's time to identify the shadows and move beyond them. You are your best asset. Your ability to choose yourself reveals to the world whether or not you believe this to be true. With this said, may the words to follow help you move from there..., for the journey to there...is expecting you!

Insight
CORNER

1. *What are some negative things that serve to contaminate your water?*

2. *What can you do to purify your content and eliminate the effects of your negative colors?*

3. *Once purified, what will you do to protect yourself from future contamination?*

From There...

What is holding you back from personal fulfillment? Yesterday. Then. The past is a great indicator of tomorrow, if we don't choose to understand it and do something different in the future. You must be willing to change, forgive, and dig beneath the surface. To move from there, you must own your reality and be honest with yourself. As you seek to grow, you must be willing to ask yourself questions and embrace the answers: Where am I? How do I feel? How did I get here? Why am I still here?

WHAT WILL YOU DO?

What will you do when it's gone?

Time spent
Been so long

Time gone
Been there so long

Time wasted
Been around so long

What will you do when it's gone?

Forget about the pain it causes
Forget about it dragging you down

Forget about the spirit lashes
Wounded spaces
Life turned upside down

But what will you do when it's gone?

Is that why you let it hang around so long?
Because you don't know what you'll do when it's gone?

You'll finally start to live!

Chapter 1
Losing Weight Ain't Easy

s we think of our womanly journey toward peace, balance, and purpose, we often struggle with the recognition that an overloaded spirit cannot travel at optimum efficiency. Despite this reality, time and circumstance often promote a tendency to collect people, things, and memories that represent quantity rather than quality in our lives. Instead of choosing ourselves and traveling light, many of us struggle with fear of loss and perceptions of permanence that serve to further weigh us down. Like moving to a new apartment or home, everything in our current residence will not be moved to the next location. Some things need to be disposed of, given away, or simply left behind. As you pack boxes for the transition, it's up to you to evaluate each object's importance as it relates to the vision of your new home. This process offers an exercise in removal versus accumulation.

For many of us, packing offers a needed opportunity to assess the value and utility of items acquired throughout the years. This effort helps to identify items that have claimed space because of past need rather than present usefulness. However, the logical nature of this process does not eliminate the battle for what should stay and what should go. For example, there are at least fifteen pairs of shoes I never, I mean never wear, but I can't seem to give them away. These shoes have graced my closet for such a long time that most have become permanent fixtures. When I purchased each pair, I justified my ownership, but, as time passed, my inability to use them did not prompt my getting rid of them. I was afraid of change.

As we move toward embracing the premise of choosing ourselves, the word *change* becomes inescapable. Despite our need for familiarity, each metaphoric move from one place to another screams that a transformation is necessary. Sometimes the move requires that we alter our perceptions, disposition, expectations, and attitude. In general, choosing ourselves imparts an individual responsibility to seek people, places, and things that work to reinforce our personal empowerment, fulfillment, and purpose. Therein, one aspect of choosing ourselves suggests a continuous cleanup of life space. In doing so, we must recognize, challenge, and eliminate elements that occupy our lives just because of time spent, familiarity, or fear. Without this process, the accumulation of deadweight becomes inevitable.

This excess weight is counterproductive at best. For example, think of yourself on a rowboat carrying 250 pounds of useless cargo. If nothing else were predictable, you could almost guarantee that this type of cargo would promote a strenuous and seemingly impossible journey. In theory, throwing the items overboard would be a simple solution. However, losing weight is never easy. Freedom from unproductive relationships, jobs, criticism, and experiences that weigh us down is no simple task. Losing it is not easy and the identification of it can be a catastrophic process within itself. It takes courage to identify it and even more courage to do something about it. Choosing yourself demands that you stop and acknowledge the need to shed excess weight, or at minimum, render it powerless. Allowing people and things to coexist with you, despite the ill effects on your personal growth and happiness, is not healthy. If something consistently puts you in a negative space or someone is rarely positive, selfless, or constructive toward you, it's time to make a change. It's time to start traveling light.

This premise suggests that nothing and no one be allowed to be in your life for the sheer purpose of occupancy. If you don't ascribe to this, you go against the notion that you deserve to surround yourself with people, places, and things that are good to and for you. In essence, everyone and everything should earn his space. Anything else equates to settling for less than you deserve.

As women, we cannot afford occupancy that unnecessarily weighs us down. Ignoring the reality that deadweight is harmful does not make it harmless. It leads to the promotion of stress, exhaustion, and low self-esteem while serving to overshadow and influence the very nature of personal fulfillment. Why? Because the excess occupies space that would normally be used more efficiently. So, as we venture to travel light we must acknowledge five simple truths: 1) people's actions speak louder than their words, 2) each of us has the right to protect our time and choose to spend it with people who appreciate and respect it, 3) our gut instinct deserves to be listened to and revered, 4) anyone or anything that creates more discomfort and sadness than joy needs to be removed, and 5) the wholeness of who you are is defined by only you.

The avoidance of these truths often aid in justifying and prolonging the unnecessary load most of us carry. It is not unusual for us to cling to people's words and ignore their actions. As some of us struggle with fears of being wronged, misunderstood, or judged, many of us simply ignore how some people make us feel. We often fight against our gut instinct as if it were the enemy. To add insult to injury, many of us willingly move toward symbolically glaring red lights while pretending they are green. For example, I once had a job interview with a hiring manager who gave me a bad feeling. However, I let myself be convinced that I was being ridiculous and accepted the position when it was offered. From the first day of employment to the last, my gut instinct was reaffirmed. The anger and frustration I experienced with this boss proved that I should have left that interview and run as far away from that job as I could when I had the chance. But I didn't respect my instinct enough to accept what it was saying.

A similar scenario happened a couple of years later, but this time I listened. Though initially excited about a leadership position at a major corporation, I refused to accept a third interview within the hiring process because I perceived the situation to be potential for deadweight. This time around, I could not let the salary, title, or promise of career advancement persuade me that my gut was saying move forward, when in reality, it was telling me that the opportunity was not right for me. This time, my intuition was telling me to stop, and I followed it. I chose myself and decided to listen rather than ignore the voice that often had insight beyond the obvious.

In addition to ignoring our intuition, many of us retain relationships with people who are bona fide takers. These people rarely give and suck the energy out of most people with whom they come in contact. In fact, they fit the criteria perfectly. No matter how much we try to justify their presence in our lives, they often promote feelings of deficiency rather than rejuvenation. When we allow them to be an intricate part of our lives, we ignore our need for balance. Like bank accounts, we, too, become unbalanced when there are steady withdrawals without deposits. Harboring these people in our lives is just as burdensome as defining who we are by the standards of others instead of our own. Choosing yourself requires that you create and live up to our own expectations. You are the only person who needs to define you. Self-definition is a power that you own unless you accept the deadweight of letting the expectations of others run your life.

So, it's time to throw the heavy cargo overboard! You may decide to walk away, say good-bye, or just be open to the truth as it presents itself, but action is required. Although some of your weight-loss process may begin immediately, others may take a bit more time, planning, and execution. A young lady I met recently decided to start college at the age of thirty-one. Her decision was an attempt to lose the deadweight of an unfulfilling job and gain financial flexibility and fulfillment within a new career. Although in the short term her decision to obtain a college degree was challenging, the long-term effort was necessary to release the weight that was hindering her personal growth. She made a conscious decision to lose the weight and inadvertently moved toward gaining muscle. Her actions embraced what I call the Muscle Challenge: a conscious decision to seek and retain fruitful friendships; work within equally yoked or equally compatible romantic relationships; spend time based on personal choice; and surround oneself with resources, people, and things that promote personal enhancement.

Muscle is the best replacement for deadweight because it creates a stronger, happier, and healthier sense of self. Muscle works for, rather than against, you. It builds strength, endurance, and confidence while promoting the use of tools like honesty, love, and determination to maintain a sense of personal freedom and liberation. So, if you still question what you will do when the weight is gone, remember, clutter never affords much room for openings, opportunities, or blessings that may be waiting to be a breath of fresh air in your life. No matter how you slice it, deadweight is a liability. The decision to perceive the release of it as an opportunity to spread your wings and live a more content and fulfilling life is a choice.

Insight
CORNER

1. Who and what can be characterized as deadweight in your life?

2. Why do you consider those items to be deadweight?

3. Why do you think you hold on to the weight that you've identified?

4. What would happen if you decided to remove the deadweight from your life?

_____

_____

_____

_____

_____

_____

_____

_____

_____

_____

_____

_____

_____

_____

_____

_____

_____

_____

_____

_____

_____

_____

_____

_____

_____

_____

_____

_____

5. *What will you do to remove or minimize the weight?*

6. When will you start the removal process?

a. How will you do it?

b. How will you keep yourself accountable to the decision of removal and plans of action?

7. Once the deadweight is removed, how will you build muscle in your life?

a. What new or unused resources will you tap into?

Nicole LaBeach

b. With what type of people or places will you seek to surround yourself?

c. What new opportunities/activities will you embrace?

WITH REVERENCE

As I look at your face
Your beauty astounds me

Your smiles bring joy
Your eyes share wisdom
And your hugs

Your hugs are like chocolate…

After a month of dieting

You are my confidant
My friend
And my muse

Your views nurtured my thoughts
And
Your sacrifice taught me the "rules"

The rules of womanhood

Watching you helped to define the me I've come to be

Our friendship brings new meaning to the word *love*
You've been a God-given navigator of my journey
A human shield to cover me
All for one purpose
The purpose of helping me realize my potential

Now I understand!

What greater gift than the love of a mother?
What greater thanks than the admiration of a daughter?

Chapter 2
The Woman She Is,
The Lessons She Gives

*B*eing a woman is no easy task. The very nature of womanhood is complex and the full-proof recipe for happiness has yet to be published. Maybe it's because happiness in its true essence is subjective. Despite its subjectivity, some of us still struggle with the term *happiness* because we regard it as an accidental circumstance rather than a deserved disposition or better yet, we don't know how to achieve it. As a result, many of us have been taught to believe that happiness is something to be yearned for but never truly realized. As women, we have even learned that true happiness is usually achieved at the expense of something or someone. Well, this premise is true. Not realizing and owning the right to be happy does come at someone's expense: your own. Instead of seeking fulfillment, we have embraced the mundane and accepted that we may never experience contentment for long periods. Instead, we wake up and go to sleep wanting more for our lives while being bogged down by our personal baggage. Part of releasing our baggage comes from choosing ourselves through making an honest assessment of significant relationships and lessons learned within them. This chapter and the next touch on two influential people in most of our lives: our mothers (mother figures) and fathers (father figures).

It is fair to say that experiences from significant relationships create a symbolic road or pattern we tend to follow. Much of this road is created and paved through our childhood and adolescence. These years provide many bearers of knowledge. One of the master teachers during this time is clearly our mother or mother figure. Her influence on our womanhood is undeniable. Some of the finest lessons in choosing and not choosing yourself came from what you learned within this relationship. In general, the mother-daughter dynamic is quite complex. In fact, it's probably one of the most complex that girls experience because it symbolically represents a vertical relationship (one in which you—the daughter—look up to her—the mother—to help define your sense of self). Though this may take a minute or two to digest, it's true. Your mother, like it or not, has often been used as the frame of reference from which you could freely compare your own growth and maturity. Both consciously and subconsciously, she created a template that served to exemplify the "shoulds" and "shouldn'ts" of life. In every sense of the word, she represented power in its most natural state: power by way of influence. Her presence (or lack thereof) is likened to the pruning of a tree.

Like a tree, part of our womanly essence is determined by the care she gave and the life she lived. When absent or dysfunctional, the yearning for or adoption of another is likened to the struggle a plant endures when it tries to survive with little or no care. Good, bad, or indifferent, your mother imparted value systems that were eventually held as rules to live by or stray from. Some of us hate to admit it, but we've all compared ourselves to our mother. Some of us want to be just like her, and others want to be nothing like her, but whether we love, hate, don't understand, or don't know her, the comparison is inevitable. And, rarely can we dissect our personal character without considering her effect on our lives.

For most of us, our mother's guidance served as footprints to move us toward womanhood. As many of us seek to live healthier lives, we have no choice but to question from where some of our initial lessons in not choosing ourselves came. Chances are many of these lessons were learned from your mother. As you think back, do you remember her having a sense of personal fulfillment? If your definition of her happiness was characterized by the ability to be all things to all people, you are not alone. Though some of us had varying definitions, many of us still have mental snapshots of our mother's experiences, struggles, and choices. These snapshots prompted us to vow to never do certain things like her. The serious declaration "I will never do...like my mother" is one to pay close attention to in the choosing yourself journey. Women from all walks of life have made this statement on different occasions. While ignoring the implication of this statement, many of us have failed to recognize that the declaration itself is either connected to hurtful memories or a change in personal values. As a result, few of us have given intense thought to the items placed on the infamous never-to-do list.

I challenge you to ask yourself: What have I vowed to never do like my mother? This list may take a while for you to create. When you answer this question in the Insight Corner you may find that you've created a list that's a bit long, but it won't get you struck down by lightning, I promise. Whether your mother is a grand image you hold near and dear, or one you try to forget, serious thought toward this question tends to reveal significant baggage that often goes unrecognized. Why? Believe it or not, most of the items on this list highlight your mother's inability to choose and regard herself. And, as you further dissect your list, you will find that as daughters, it's not enough to just say you "will never." First, you must explore why you put each item on your list. Second, you must question why doing them would be such a wrong choice. Third, you must choose to acknowledge any similarities between your past and present choices and her experiences. Finally, you must make the necessary changes to stop repeating the same patterns you've vowed to abandon.

Even with the most honorable intentions, mothers have often ignored that it's very difficult for a daughter to "do as I say and not as I do." It's amazing because I still call my mother and discuss past incidents that leave her a bit surprised at how carefully I audited her every move. For me, she was the blueprint from which I polished my personal masterpiece—me. Like many of you, I learned a great deal from my mother. However, I also struggled to avoid some of her behaviors that I perceived as being negative. As I created and edited my personal list, I found an overarching theme: My mother was a consummate self-sacrificer. This role was quite challenging for me because I viewed it as one that worked to the detriment of her emotions, physical health, and ultimate happiness. As I looked at my list, I saw various items that brought on feelings of betrayal to the wonderful woman she was, and is, but I had to keep digging beneath the surface. Being open (as I am challenging you to be), I offer a personal example that I hope will help you to see how I dissected one of my personal never-to-do items. It is my hope that this example will help you explore the things that you've placed on your own list.

One of the items on my never-to-do list was a vow to never have a marriage like my parents. If you asked what was wrong with their marriage, I would offer the following statement: My father was a terrible husband. At first glance, you may have noticed that this assessment conveniently excluded my mother. Now please believe me when I tell you life was never quite the same when I realized that she, too, should have been part of that statement. As I tried to evaluate my parents' marriage, I had to ask, could my father have been a good husband for someone else and just not a good match for my mother? Answering this question meant one of two things: My mother either chose the wrong man or chose what she thought was the right man and decided to stay even when she figured out she was wrong!

Either answer resulted in the reality that my mother elected to stay in an unfulfilling situation for more than thirty years rather than choose to remove herself and be liberated from it. The realization that my mother may have perpetuated her own unhappiness was initially overwhelming. Like many mothers, she loved her child, husband, home, friends, relatives, and job more than she loved herself. This was painful to admit. However, as I further dissected this situation, I started to see some similarities between her personal life decisions and my own. In fact, this item red-flagged my own personal tolerance in relationships. It helped me see how what I had previously justified as the behavior of a "good girlfriend" was really the continuation of a cycle that dishonored the right to choose myself. My mother didn't choose herself in her relationship, and I was traveling down the same path.

Without previously connecting the dots, I, too, developed staying power in situations that were stagnant, debilitating, and unfulfilling. Dysfunction had become a familiar expectation. When I asked myself why, I recognized my feelings of insecurity. Though I desired the love experienced in a functional relationship, I didn't feel worthy of it. Being in a functional commitment was unfamiliar territory, too unfamiliar to bare. In a strange sort of way, I developed a craving for dysfunctional situations. While in these relationships, I was too afraid to just walk away. I couldn't just quit "cold turkey" because termination would have denied me my fix (the satisfaction of my self-defeating needs). Like my mother, I would temporarily leave and then return with a good excuse justifying why the relationship needed to work.

I would describe my mother as an independent, intelligent, and accomplished woman. Why would this type of woman remain in a situation that represented a broken covenant, lack of support, and the hindrance of growth? I had to pose that question to myself. As I pondered her motive, I realized my mother learned early in life that commitment, accountability, and reciprocation were not always a part of the relationship bargain. Devoid of decisions made, circumstances experienced, and a worn spirit, she was determined to stay. It occurred to me that my mother did not learn to receive, she only valued herself through giving. Despite the woman she was, she had yet to truly recognize her value. As a result, she endured a spiritually and emotionally debilitating situation spanning over thirty years.

As I was knee deep in the discovery triggered by this one item, I had two choices: turn back and run for cover, or keep going and make some real progress. I chose the latter. Once I swallowed the fact that my past relationships were not that different from hers, I had to let my mother off the hook (for what I learned from her) and put myself on it. Besides imitating what I saw, what exactly did I get out of these experiences? Then, it hit me like a ton of bricks: I perceived leaving as failure. My unhealthy relationships were not just acceptable because of familiarity; they were appealing because they reduced my fear of failure. What would I have done with someone who hated arguing, took responsibility for his actions, and wanted to have a content situation? Nothing. That person presented no challenge. With people I could fix, I felt triumphant. Fixing the situation was my drug of choice. It made me feel valuable, powerful, and in control. It never occurred to me the cost of engaging in these relationships was me. I underestimated my worth, which caused me to hide in unions that did nothing to illuminate my worth. It became clear that my fear of inadequacy caused me to date people who never should have been considered as intimate partners.

As you will find when you go through your list, you, too, will gain insight that may put you in an uneasy place, one in which you become keenly aware of your own reality. As you, too, may discover in your own journey, I came across information that revealed I needed to save myself from my own hand of destruction. So now what? Once I had this information I had to figure out what to do with it. First and foremost, I stopped dating for a while and made a firm decision to not revisit the old relationships that were previous revolving doors. I took the time to think about what made me feel devalued, powerless, and out of control in the first place. I had to search for the origin of these feelings. Then I had to choose to try and make myself the gauge of my own value, power, and control. After staying out of the dating game for a significant amount of time, I was able to gauge my re-entrance by my readiness for companionship rather than a need for validation. I changed my dating criteria and embraced experiences that respected my right to choose myself. In other words, I listened to my intuition and terminated situations that were not good to or for me.

As I journeyed through the rest of my never-to-do list, I treated everything as a possible learning point. When I was done, the insight

I gained was life changing. As I viewed every item, I was able to look at my mother and myself in the same mirror. I chose myself by embracing her past as insight toward the choices I had made, was making, and would be likely to make if I didn't make healthier decisions. This process forced me to recognize that her experiences did have an impact on what I accepted, repeated, and rejected in my own womanhood. For most, this exercise promises to be exhausting if taken seriously, but the reality is we can either choose to embrace opportunities for insight or shy away from them. As you identify ways in which you have exhibited the same undesirable behaviors and decisions as your mother, it's up to you to challenge yourself and figure out what you personally received from these experiences. When you decipher the needs and fears that were perpetuated in your own choices, it's up to you to make the necessary changes. As you challenge yourself through this exercise, burdens will be lifted and clarity will abound.

In hindsight, I acknowledge that this process felt horrible at first, but it ultimately served to help both my mother and me grow. I received a sense of freedom and boldness that words cannot describe. This part of the journey was so liberating, I decided to share it with the person needing to hear it the most, my mother. A year and a half later with strength and courage (surpassed by few in my mind), she made the choice to change her marital status. For the first time in years, she embraced the right to choose herself.

For many mothers, their greatest wish is that their children enjoy "a life that doesn't experience the same pain or repeat the same mistakes, but one that symbolizes fulfillment and happiness at its best." It is my hope that this chapter moves you one step closer toward this wish come true.

Insight
CORNER

1. How would you describe the relationship between you and your mother/mother figure?

a. What kind of woman is/was she?

_____

_____

_____

_____

_____

_____

_____

_____

_____

_____

_____

_____

_____

_____

_____

_____

_____

_____

_____

_____

_____

_____

_____

_____

_____

_____

_____

_____

b. *Do you see much of her (mannerisms, likes/dislikes, personality) in the person that you are? If so, how? If not, why?*

_____

_____

_____

_____

_____

_____

_____

_____

_____

_____

_____

_____

_____

_____

_____

_____

_____

_____

_____

_____

_____

_____

_____

2. *In the left column list the things you wanted to do or have done like your mother/mother figure. In the right column name some things you have vowed to never do like your mother/mother figure.*

THINGS TO EMULATE   THINGS TO NEVER DO

_____ _____

_____ _____

_____ _____

_____ _____

_____ _____

_____ _____

_____ _____

_____ _____

_____ _____

_____ _____

_____ _____

_____ _____

_____ _____

_____ _____

_____ _____

_____ _____

_____ _____

_____ _____

3. Examining each item, why would doing each thing listed in the right column be so terrible?

_____

_____

_____

_____

_____

_____

_____

_____

_____

_____

_____

_____

_____

_____

_____

_____

_____

_____

_____

_____

_____

_____

_____

4. *Despite the items listed in the right column, do you find yourself engaging in similar behaviors? If so, how do your behaviors or decisions seem similar?*

_____

_____

_____

_____

_____

_____

_____

_____

_____

_____

_____

_____

_____

_____

_____

_____

_____

_____

_____

_____

_____

_____

_____

_____

_____

5. *How have the never-to-do items affected your sense of emotional, spiritual, and physical fulfillment?*

6. Thinking in terms of needs and fulfillment as they relate to the never-to-do items that you have emulated, what was the motive behind your behaviors?

a. What did you receive as a result of your actions/decisions? What was in it for you?

b. What void(s) were you trying to fill as a result of your actions/decisions?

_____

_____

_____

_____

_____

_____

_____

_____

_____

_____

_____

_____

_____

_____

_____

_____

_____

_____

_____

_____

_____

_____

_____

_____

_____

c. What fears were being sheltered or avoided as a result of your actions/decisions?

_____

_____

_____

_____

_____

_____

_____

_____

_____

_____

_____

_____

_____

_____

_____

_____

_____

_____

_____

_____

_____

_____

_____

_____

7. *What will you do to stop the repetitive cycle from being perpetuated? How will you stay accountable to this decision?*

THE FIRST KNIGHT

Dare to raise your daughter
That she may know her worth

Mothers can't deny their purpose
But you, father,
Are yearned from birth

Your daughters will marry one like you
Your sons will mirror the image you drew
For sons, the need is evident
For daughters, the need, more intricate

To her, you are the first true knight
Your love like oxygen
Your words like the gospel
Your presence like the sun

Your actions will define her views
Your laughter will bring her joy
Your attention will minimize her doubts
Your time will set many standards

Dare to raise your daughter
It's clear that you're in need

And surely it's apparent you'll help predict
the kind of life she'll lead

Chapter 3
A New Season

For every woman, a strong and positive father figure is truly worth his weight in gold. In society, the role of motherhood has received consistent attention. A mother's physical, emotional, and spiritual commitment to the nurturing of her children is often praised and held in high regard. However, the importance of the father to the psychological prosperity of his children is often ignored and denied. For men, the father/son relationship, like the mother/daughter dynamic, is very similar. Intuitively, boys look to their fathers for guidance on how to become men. The importance of fathers to their sons is not surprising but the significance of fathers to their daughters is consistently underrated. As girls, we experience an intricate bond with our fathers. We look to our mothers for an indication of who we will become and how we should conduct ourselves. However, fathers introduce how to interact with and be loved by the opposite sex. As a result, many women's romantic experiences reflect attributes learned from the father/daughter relationship.

When positive, the father/daughter bound is one of the safest places to learn how to be treated. It teaches us how to accept ourselves, feel deserving of love, and give love. Its impact is evidenced in many different aspects of our personal and professional lives. If you are the recipient of a positive father-daughter relationship, it is difficult to overlook this value in your life. A father's smiles, hugs, confidence boosts, talks, compliments, financial support, discipline, and dedication all work together to nurture a subconscious sense of security and conscious sense of worth. His example helps to validate that you deserve to be provided for, treated with respect, and held in high regard. Men who provide this for their daughters are rarely celebrated and are often overshadowed, though they are priceless. These men deserve a phone call to thank them for a relationship that mirrored the tenets of love, honor, and respect. For those who have passed on, they deserve to have an honored memory and to be acknowledged for setting standards their daughters could proudly expect others to meet. Though not perfect, these men should be admired for their ability to protect as well as save the day. Their emotional availability and physical presence indirectly set the bar for what should be expected, accepted, and received by their daughters. Fathers' acceptance and commitment has long-term effects. These efforts often materialize in a high propensity for positive friendships, intimate relationships, and personal standards on the part of their daughters.

In my experiences, I've found that women who perceive strong, positive, and functional relationships with their fathers exhibit less insecurity, more optimism, and more options that choose themselves. By no means do these women have perfect lives, perfect encounters with romantic partners, or even the portrayal of a perfect childhood. However, their positive father/daughter connection does provide them with less emotional baggage and prepares them to create and maintain more healthy situations with others. For most of these women, this connection was nurtured by three things: their father's commitment to the responsibilities of fatherhood; his positive treatment of their mother; and his ability to give, receive, and exemplify love and respect toward them. Consequently, emotional baggage often originates from deficiencies in one or all of these areas. The significance of these circumstances within our growth helps to explain why a negative father/daughter dynamic has the power to inflict gaping wounds to our self-esteem and sense of worth. In fact, as the relationship grows in a dysfunctional direction, it fosters expertise in collecting and reinforcing negative feelings that bleed into the rest of our lives.

When a father is emotionally unavailable, avoidant of the teacher role, or absent, the consequences are critical. As little girls, we may miss, yearn for, or recognize the void, however, the reality of how crucial this relationship is to our esteem is slow to be realized. The impact of dysfunctions within this dynamic often lay dormant until a girl enters late adolescence or adulthood. Our insight toward its effect often gains momentum when we start to relate to others intimately, define our roles within, and seek validation from the opposite sex. For many, negativity in this relationship is a great predictor of problems in future situations because it often fosters cycles of insecurity, pain, and anger, all of which can only be overcome by a desire and willingness to heal.

For many of us, healing can be a battle of wills: the will to stay angry versus the will to be free. Though this statement is hard for many women to admit, choosing ourselves requires healing of the father/daughter bond as an absolute necessity rather than luxury. In my personal journey, the battle toward resolved feelings for my father was unlike anything I had ever experienced. Resolution within this relationship presented one of life's ultimate ironies: forgiveness for someone for whom I felt hurt feelings.

In my childhood, I had fond memories of my father, however, the closer I moved toward adolescence, the more my loving and respectful ideals of him seemed to fall apart. With maturity, I began to see how much he struggled with his role as a father and husband. More specifically, I saw how difficult it was for my father to provide a sense of trust, security, and stability for our family. The consequences of his choices were often painful, long lasting, and unforgettable. Throughout my adolescent struggle to give him the benefit of the doubt, my allegiance eventually turned to disappointment, disrespect, and disdain. I resented him for not being the man I once perceived. In my eyes, he made our lives unnecessarily difficult and failed to go the extra mile to care for our needs. As time progressed, we talked less and argued more. While our relationship fell apart, my mind questioned what was wrong with him as my heart wondered what was wrong with me. The more I identified my worth by his choices, the more devastated I became. With every spin, this cycle of pain served to push my father and me to what I thought was the brink of no return.

Like many women, I dealt with the intensity of my feelings through the mastery of illusion. I convinced myself my issues with my father didn't affect me, matter, or mean anything. However, the reality of this façade always surfaced when I attempted to have an intimate relationship. Without fail, all my relational experiences served to intensify my unresolved feelings toward him. My emotional unavailability, combativeness, and fear of vulnerability were the tell-tale signs that something was seriously wrong.

Quite frankly, I wish I could say resolution was something I just decided to embrace on a warm summer day. The truth is, my unresolved issues left me emotionally paralyzed. As it related to my father, I had decided that the hurt he caused didn't deserve to be forgiven. For many of us, we have convinced ourselves that forgiveness denounces our pain and somehow endorses wrongdoing. As a result, it takes a long time for us to recognize that the price of resolution is far less than the price of continued avoidance. It takes even longer for us to see it as an act of choosing ourselves. Though risky and uncomfortable, the quest for resolution in this and every other relationship deserves as much energy as the negativity that often discourages you from it. As with the father/daughter bond, there are a myriad of circumstances that create valid justifications for our anger, indifference, and unforgiveness. These circumstances often range from their irreconcilable differences with our mothers to being unprepared for fatherhood. These justifications often serve to encourage the notion that forgiveness is a sole gift to him rather than a gift to ourselves. This premise alone makes resolution seem impossible, however, we cannot ignore the outcome of intense negativity toward our fathers: the inabilities to give love, receive love, or be understood beyond the superficial.

For those of you who don't buy into the rationale that resolution within this relationship is important, I challenge you to give the premise more consideration. In recognizing that none of us can reverse the hands of time, redo, or erase the past, resolution is the best any of us can hope to achieve. Without negating the fact that some father-daughter relationships represent a plethora of thoughts and feelings, the fact still remains, choosing ourselves and realizing our potential is dependent on our ability to thrive, which is dependent on our emulation of love. And, our ability to emulate love is directly connected to our ability to forgive.

As it relates to negative feelings toward others, we have the choice to forgive and have a sense of peace or we can be unforgiving and experience the deep sadness, anger, and resentment that accompany this option. However, when we attempt to deny negative feelings from significant relationships like that between fathers and daughters, we rarely disguise what is being felt or internalized. At best, we can only hope to fool ourselves. Chances are, any person of significance in our intimate history can identify behaviors prompted by the negativity or absence of the father/daughter relationship. Though we continue to try, few of us have been successful at hiding the emotional seeds planted by this bond or the lack thereof. If you don't believe me, go to the first question in this chapter's Insight Corner and write down the names of your closest girlfriends. Put an X by the ones raised without their father's influence, two X's by those who were raised within a strained father/daughter relationship, and put three X's by those who were raised by and seem to have strong and healthy interactions with their fathers. Now, look at the names that have three X's. What type of men do they appear to attract? What type of relationships do they seem to have? What type of disposition do they have toward relationships? I'll bet they act and appear to perceive things differently than the other women on your list. Part of this disparity pertains to what I call "daddy baggage." We all have a "daddy bag" but it's not the bag that presents the problem, it's the content. It's like the difference between traveling with a suitcase full of coordinated outfits (the father/daughter relationship built on a strong foundation of love, respect, and consistency) versus one full of clothes that don't match, need alterations, and don't compliment your shoes. For the most part, the content either promotes a sense of confidence and preparedness or anxiety and fear.

This concept was reaffirmed through a conversation I had with one of my close male friends. He said that as a single, intelligent, and financially successful male, he meets his fair share of single women. He noted that he had to be very careful because some of these women portrayed themselves to be secure individuals, which was often untrue. As I listened, he clearly articulated his frustration with "daddy baggage" that made it difficult to experience a functional and non-contentious relationship with these women. Without knowing it, he suggested a woman's feelings toward her father are revered, resolved, or suppressed. If in fact her feelings are suppressed and unresolved, the resulting residue usually rears its ugly head at some point in other situations.

In conjunction with affecting success within relationships, the father/daughter dynamic also helps to create what you might call the "invisible billboard." This theory suggests that people are often drawn together by figurative advertisements: verbal and nonverbal communication of personal boundaries (what you will and won't do) and baggage (what you've experienced and not resolved) that either attracts people to you or repels them from you. Whether positive or negative, the father/daughter relationship often affects the information we send out to those we encounter. For example, a woman who has witnessed abuse at the hands of her father is more likely to exemplify an ad of questionable self-worth, past experiences of violence, and patterns of dependence than one who hasn't. This type of ad would be very attractive to a man who has a disposition to abuse women and prey on their insecurities.

We can either choose to move toward a place of resolution (forgiveness and peace) with our fathers or we can suffer the pain-filled consequences and limitations. Our ability to confront denial, sadness, and unmet needs gives us the best chance to not relive those issues in our future. In this regard, we are required to own our feelings, acknowledge painful memories, and embrace the power of letting go. Doing so will move you closer to attracting and maintaining healthy and more fulfilling connections. It will allow you to see opportunities clearly and afford you the option of being emotionally, physically, and mentally present, devoid of unnecessary baggage.

For me, the resolution I experienced with my father changed my demeanor and made me free to embrace my potential for happiness. I know it's hard to admit that scared and hurt little girls can grow up to be scared and hurt women, but it's often a predictable truth. You cannot erase the past, and you may not be able to create a new relationship with your father, but you can refuse to further embrace an avoidant or wounded existence. This does not mean you should close your eyes to the man your father was, is, or isn't, but it does mean you have to make a choice to forgive or at a minimum, put the relationship in perspective. Letting go of unfulfilled expectations, broken promises, and parental inadequacies is no easy task, however, your quest for wholeness and fulfillment depends on it.

Though a negative father/daughter relationship will never determine how much you deserve to be loved, it can debilitate your ability to choose yourself and embrace the notion of love. If you look beyond your anger, you will see that forgiveness is a priceless gift in loving yourself. When I let go of the negativity that tried to take root in my heart, I was able to see my father. As I looked beyond my anger, I saw a man who experienced an intense amount of pain and one who needed to forgive himself and experience love. I recognized that his behavior in part was an extension of what he learned, yearned for, and endured throughout his lifetime. On my own volition I had to make the choice to choose myself, accept him for who he is, and refuse to continue being bitter.

Shortly after I resolved my issues with my father, we mutually agreed to work on reconciliation. After a great deal of honesty, humility, and compassion, we now talk to, laugh with, and respect each other. We started over and both of us appreciate how fortunate we are to have a second chance at love in this relationship. However, I must specify that there is a major difference between reconciliation, which is a collaborative effort (we) and resolution, which is a solo effort (I). When I sought to resolve my father/daughter baggage, I did so without any permission, help, or cooperation from my dad. He was not a factor in my ability to successfully resolve my feelings for him. Our reconciliation was not a condition of my resolution because the ability to achieve resolution is not dependent on another person's behavior, it is an individual decision that depends on one person— you. As difficult as it may be to accept, resolution is all about extending forgiveness, altering expectations, and settling for nothing less than health for ourselves. Choosing ourselves in this relationship is essential, the past may have been difficult but moving forward is critical. Now, it's up to you to take the steps to do so.

Insight
CORNER

1. Write down the names of your closest girlfriends.

_____

_____

_____

_____

_____

_____

_____

_____

_____

_____

_____

_____

_____

_____

_____

_____

_____

_____

a) *Put an X by the names of those raised without their father's influence.*

b) *Put two X's by those who were raised within a strained father/daughter relationship.*

c) *Put three X's by those who were raised by and seem to have strong and healthy relationships with their fathers.*

d) *Now, look at the names that have three X's. Think about the type of men they attract, the type of relationships they have, and the disposition they have toward relationships. You will probably see a difference between them and your other friends.*

2. *What was the relationship like between your mother and father/father figure?*

3. *What kind of man is/was your father/father figure?*

4. *Did you want him to be someone other than who he was? If so, what kind of man did you want him to be (e.g., kinder, more supportive, more active in his role as a father, etc.)?*

5. *What type of relationship do you have with your father/father figure?*

a. *If the relationship is/was positive, what can you do to acknowledge what his presence meant to you?*

b. *If it is not positive, what type of feelings does it elicit (e.g., ambivalence, negativity, or sadness)? If so, why?*

_____

_____

_____

_____

_____

_____

_____

_____

_____

_____

_____

_____

_____

_____

_____

_____

_____

_____

_____

_____

_____

_____

_____

_____

_____

6. What is the basis of these negative feelings? What happened?

a. *What impact has the relationship had on you (e.g., diminished confidence, self-worth, etc.)?*

7. *What would happen if you decided to acknowledge, purge, and let go of those negative feelings?*

_____

_____

_____

_____

_____

_____

_____

_____

_____

_____

_____

_____

_____

_____

_____

_____

_____

_____

_____

_____

_____

_____

_____

_____

8. *What will you do to forgive yourself for enduring lack of resolution for so long?*

9. *What will you do to move toward forgiving him and releasing the negativity?*

COULD IT BE?

It's something about the way I feel when looking at your smile
It's not the way you dress
Though exuding style and masculinity

It's not the way you walk
With strength and clarity of purpose

Every time I'm with you
I wonder what it is

When you hold my hand
I feel connected to the possibility of life to come and a rested spirit
I feel your desire to provide for me
Provide with me

When you move your mouth to speak
I hinge on every word
For what you speak stimulates me

Your vision and attentiveness to my thoughts
simply astounds me
Ambitious and intelligent to name a few
You hear my fears and applaud my strengths
I shudder to think that it's love

But if not, what?

Your thoughts
That of a man well traveled in self
Unashamed of questions for which you have no answers

You hold me close and for once there's quiet
With your hand on my back and my head on your chest
I can feel your humanity
That of a beating heart that's been bruised
Bruised by the cruelty of others

I know
And I thank you for letting me lay close enough to hear
And feel the reality behind your smile

Still you smile
When I talk, you smile
When I strut, you smile
When I dance, you smile
For all those things your smile matches mine
But
When I hurt, you smile
And when I'm burdened, you smile

Each time looking into my eyes with a sense of pride that
You are not the cause of my tears
Not the cause of my pain
Not the element of my weary shoulders

Then
Your spirit to mine, I heard:
Lean your chest near my heart and meet your eyes with mine
You wonder why I smile?
I smile because
I believe I can dry your tears
Ease the pain you feel
And lift your heavy disappointments

You are my queen
And I want nothing less than to be your king
Now sleep and take comfort in the quiet
I promise myself
You will never yearn for silence again.

Ready for love?
Undoubtedly.

Ready to love?
Absolutely.

Chapter 4
To Be Ready Is Very Necessary!

*M*any people suggest that fulfillment requires the embracing of goals, desires, dreams, and aspirations. Additionally, the realization of these elements require some level of being prepared for moments that will bring them to fruition. Being ready when opportunity knocks is half the battle. Although preparation does not always guarantee success, the lack of it often promotes failure. This premise lends itself to many aspects of our lives, including the achievement of positive connections within relationships. In an ironic sense, fulfillment and connection are related. Fulfillment promotes a sense of wholeness (physical, spiritual, and emotional health) and vice versa. As whole individuals, we are more likely to attract and maintain whole partners in our lives. Without denouncing the relevance of hard work, wholeness gives us the best chance at the storybook ending most of us have committed to memory.

Like many of you, I, too, have had my share of dating challenges. As I struggled through one breakup or not-quite-it experience after another, I began to think the connection I sought was unrealistic and unattainable. The more I evaluated my relationship history, the more I recognized times when I gave too much, gave too little, sabotaged purposely, sabotaged unintentionally, and just flat out made some bad choices. For a long time, I truly believed something was wrong with the men I dated. My inability to be honest with myself reinforced my belief that I just picked the wrong guys! However, I want you to try something. Take your hand and make a fist, then use your index finger to point at something. Now, look at your hand as you point. Do you notice one finger aiming away from you and three pointing back at you? In other words, before we become quick to blame others, we must first bravely look at ourselves.

In all of my past relationships, one thing remained consistent—me. Once I acknowledged the power of my presence in these situations, I recognized none of them had a prayer of being more than posters of dysfunction. Why? At the core of my being, I was less than whole. Being less than whole made me unprepared to foster or engage in a functional and connected relationship. Why? I was unprepared to manifest the woman I wanted to be. I was not ready to love myself unconditionally, nurture my own heart daily, and choose balance consistently. As a result, I was unable to attract, receive, or succeed within the type of relationship I spent forever desiring. I wanted so much but was ready for so little. As I dissected why many of my relationships were unfulfilling, I fully embraced accountability for their successes and disasters. Though I look at each encounter as a learning experience, I often wish I didn't have to repeat the same scenarios two and three times to get the message. In my repeated efforts, I wasted time, money, and energy, with little to show for it. I misused my efforts by focusing too much on others and too little on myself. I often sought to fix others and make personal alterations to please others. Rarely, did I seek to embrace or change myself to please myself. Unfortunately, many of my repeated lessons were the result of my desire to be happy without recognizing that fulfillment in outside relationships had to start within myself.

Through painful experiences, I learned that the mathematical notion of two halves making a whole was just that, a notion. The half-and-half concept doesn't work for relationships. This epiphany forced me to see that my only true chance of getting the type of connection I wanted depended on my ability to be a whole person. Like many of my friends who were also having difficulties, I had yet to define myself for me. I had a great education, diverse friends, and ambitious career goals, but behind the suit stood a personal chaos many of us know too well.

Time and time again I sought companionship with an inability to be self-fulfilled. Although my past relationships had their good points, none of them were even close to what I thought I wanted. I use the word *thought* because the more I defined myself, the more my desires evolved. The more I focused on my personal growth, the more I realized what I thought I wanted was a bit hazy to begin with. In fact, I soon recognized what I wanted was nothing more than a manifestation of what I was told I should want. Like many of you, I was forced to acknowledge that my envisioned mate could not complement me because I had yet to figure out who I was and what made me tick. Strangely enough, this premise serves to impart hope for all of us. Hope that if we diminish our bags of fear, inferiority, and low-esteem, the romantic connection many of us desire might actually be attainable.

However, the challenge in defining what we want lies within pushing aside who our families say we should date, who our friends say we should consider, and what society says we should expect and accept. As women, defining what we want for ourselves is critical. Though some of us continue to seek relationships without a clear picture of a complementing partner, one thing will never change: The human spirit thrives on connectedness. Despite our actions, it is a major conscious and subconscious goal for all of us. However, we often choose the path of most resistance to achieve it. This is due in part to the fact that some of us still don't want to recognize that the more we connect with our own spirit, the more prepared we become to join the spirit of another. Far too many relationship disasters come from ignoring this simple fact. I have witnessed more disasters than I care to have in my mental Rolodex. I have seen more of us ignore ourselves during the quest for love than I care to admit. Many of us have minimized our boundaries, overlooked our personal rules, neglected sound advice, avoided obvious truths, and allowed our self-esteem to be destroyed, all in the mislabeled name of love.

Fortunately, love does not hold any of these requirements. True love gives enough room for us to take responsibility for ourselves by choosing ourselves. Like the heart that first pumps blood to itself then the rest of the body, it, too, identifies the necessity of caring for itself so that it may adequately do its job. In this same manner, we, too, are required to care for, love, and respect ourselves first so that we may then do the same for others. This premise does not promote neglectful selflessness. Instead, self-love employs honesty, integrity, and authenticity. It also affords an appreciation of what we see as our present self requiring that we love that reflection unconditionally. It promotes that you embrace who you are in addition to who you were and who you want to be. Herein lies the irony: Who you are (present) rather than who you want to be (future growth and maturity) is often the predictor of who you attract. With this in mind, you can't help but wonder whether you are prepared to attract, receive, and maintain the type of person you want in your life. More simply, are you prepared to be seriously considered for, receive the responsibilities of, and maintain the individual balance needed to work within a functional relationship?

As I mentioned in Chapter 3, when I spoke of the invisible billboard, some of us may be masters of wearing the metaphoric mask (the one that portrays us as being free of heavy emotional baggage), but many of us are only fooling ourselves. Why? Because in the romance department, much of what we try to suppress often manifests itself in behaviors that indicate what we can and cannot handle, in addition to reflecting who we really are. For example, if you desire a mate who has a presence that commands respect, a good question to ask yourself is whether you conduct your life in a manner that promotes self-respect and respect from others. Like it or not, it makes sense: Attracting the type of mate you want does relate to your ability to foster and nurture complementary qualities within yourself.

Of course the opposites-attract theory is still evident, but when you really get down to the core of many successful relationships, similarities and complementary attributes remain. Unlike a fling or casual dating situation, once the physical attraction is surpassed, true connections manifest from work done before we meet the person. This type of work promotes a sense of preparation, confidence, and humility. I found that the closer I moved toward being the woman I wanted to be, the more I chose to pass on mates for whom I would have previously settled. Movement toward wholeness brought forth a level of honesty that made unproductive situations less tolerable. It empowered me to give the benefit of the doubt only when it seemed to be deserved, stop camouflaging my pain, and stop creating unnecessary illusions to cope. In essence, it prompted behaviors that kept my best interests at the forefront. I recognized the more we embrace our own personal truths, the more we are able to see the truth as it pertains to others. This truth renders a freedom that enables us to attract and receive love. It enables us to empower ourselves as a solo act, which increases our potential for success as part of a duo.

The more we learn to love and choose ourselves, the more we will attract people who complement our disposition. Although movement toward purpose, fulfillment, and empowerment are positive changes, those around us do not always choose to accept them. As you fight for your rightly deserved sense of wholeness, those around you (husband, boyfriend, family, friends) may resist the needed change. Let's face it, computers were a wonderful discovery, but all did not embrace the change from paper and pencil. However, despite resistance from others, you must resist the temptation to revert to previous destinations of emotional emptiness. It is up to you to acknowledge your desire for connection and understand that wholeness is one of the perks to that end.

All this being said, being ready to receive a partner with whom you can have a connected relationship is no easy task. For those of us who are dating, committed, engaged, or married, we all know this to be true. In general, wholeness in a relationship is a real challenge unto itself. How do we assert the right to choose ourselves, love someone else, and maintain the needs of the relationship at the same time? Once we are ready to love and are in a position to receive it, how do we fight off losing the essence of who we are and who we want to be?

Recently, a friend of mine debated this issue with me. She spoke of the challenge experienced between catering to her spouse's needs and her own despite being in a connected marriage. Though in love, high expectations, huge responsibilities, and tremendous guilt were all reasons she used to explain why choosing herself was almost impossible. How do we self-impose this idea? Furthermore, how do we teach others to hold tight to the expectation that we are self-replenishing machines? Though we often don't mean to, our behaviors often teach others that we don't need to choose ourselves, we can run on empty, and we rarely have personal needs. When we go through our daily lives being all things to all people with little regard for ourselves, we unintentionally show people how to disregard us.

I contend that we teach people how to treat us. Each relationship experiences moments that show us how to respond to, treat, and understand our mate, however, we often take the power of these moments for granted. As we embrace the bliss of a loving relationship, we often make the mistake of measuring our happiness solely by the happiness of our partner. I, like many others, have avoided and misused many teachable moments by choosing to be silent when I should have spoken. In many circumstances I chose to be overly agreeable rather than forthright about my likes and dislikes. I often chose to show how selfless I could be rather than how I wanted to be treated. I gave all of my time to my relationships and taught my partners that I didn't need much time for myself. I often volunteered to change my mind and my schedule to accommodate their desires, thus setting standards that dishonored choosing myself. I inadvertently presented myself as a superwoman rather than one who had clear needs and desires. Like many of us, I had to learn that my ability to maintain a connected relationship did not require that I deprive, abandon, and not attend to myself.

We all have a spirit that needs to be cared for, but we must realize the need to choose ourselves is something that has to be embraced by us and taught to our partners. In most connected partnerships, people don't intend to overlook the needs, thoughts, and desires of their mate. However, permission to do so often comes from us. If we don't take our own sense of balance seriously, neither will our mate. If we don't take personal time to nurture ourselves, no one else will demand that we do so. It is our responsibility to teach others to respect our needs with the same intensity we use to consider theirs. If we act like we don't have any needs, we create a false impression that our needs are nonexistent. So, if you are in a new relationship, you can only hurt yourself by not using some of the teachable moments to help your partner understand that you, too, must maintain your sense of wholeness.

If you've been in a relationship for a long time, you have a bit more work to do because you have to help your partner unlearn what you previously taught. Now is not the time to feel burdened and helpless. Now is the time to recognize that each day presents new opportunities to teach your mate new lessons on what you desire and deserve.

For example, if you want time for yourself, friendships, relaxation, reflection, and the like, you must first be able to clearly communicate your needs, then make and take the time to fulfill them. You cannot allow yourself to make excuses for decisions that denounce your own needs. As the debate with my friend ensued, I asked her how much time she makes to rejuvenate her spirit on a weekly basis, and she had no answer. As we both embraced her silence and nonverbal frustration, I couldn't help but remember a conversation I had with a close colleague a few weeks prior. Our conversation focused on children, romantic partnerships, and the time they require. A content mother and wife in her own right, my colleague admitted that neither relationship requires all of her time, but neither of them would refuse it if she gave it. More simply, whether single, married, parents, or both, we are the masters of our own time and must find ways to balance and nurture our own spirit within it. We must save ourselves from the mental equation that often destroys the self: all of my time plus all of my energy equals a good mother, wife, mate, and worker. This is often the expectation that makes us feel guilty, irresponsible, and selfish. And, this equation creates a tired, stressed-out, and disgruntled individual.

Being our best to our friends, family, partners, and children will never require giving everything we have to them while giving nothing to ourselves. And, disconnection from self is the surest way to be disconnected from everyone else. The fact is, when you nurture and care for yourself, you have more to give. Many of us have trained ourselves to prepare for and receive a mate, but few of us have really considered or mastered how to maintain a sense of personal growth within this relationship. No matter the circumstance, I know this to be true. Long-term maintenance requires a take-no-prisoner attitude in finding, embracing, and giving to ourselves. Indeed, there are things companionship will provide, but the foundation of love for oneself won't derive from being with someone else. As women, we must motivate and empower ourselves frequently, feed our spirits consistently, experience joy daily, forgive ourselves repeatedly, purge our pain effectively, celebrate our uniqueness habitually, and love ourselves intensely.

Our quest for wholeness requires that we move from some of our old comfort zones and create new ones that allow us to change and grow. It mandates we save ourselves from situations that are not healthy or complimentary to us. It requires we have insight about what makes us feel safe, secure, respected, and loved. In reality, having a connected relationship is not just about being chosen. It is also about being empowered enough as women to be sure the choice is mutual (your choice of a mate is just as important as your mate's choice of you). It's about loving ourselves enough to respect the qualities that promote growth and healing in our lives. It's about first being good to ourselves so that we can appropriately manifest our love for others.

Insight
CORNER

1. What does the concept of wholeness mean to you?

2. *Do you consider yourself to be a whole person (one who is experiencing a sense of physical, spiritual, and emotional balance)? If not, why?*

_____

_____

_____

_____

_____

_____

_____

_____

_____

_____

_____

_____

_____

_____

_____

_____

_____

_____

_____

_____

_____

_____

_____

_____

_____

_____

3. In a perfect situation, what qualities, behaviors, and characteristics would you look for in a mate?

4. *Why are these things important to you?*

5. Does your personal character complement the characteristics and disposition you would like in a mate? More simply, are you prepared to attract and receive this type of person in your life? If not, on what do you need to work?

_____

_____

_____

_____

_____

_____

_____

_____

_____

_____

_____

_____

_____

_____

_____

_____

_____

_____

_____

_____

_____

_____

_____

_____

_____

6. What would a connected romantic relationship look like for you?

7. *If you are presently in a relationship, does your mate respect your right to choose yourself? If not, what has given you that impression?*

a. Have you used the teachable moments of your relationship to introduce, promote, and reinforce the need to choose yourself? If not, what will you do to start doing do so?

_____

_____

_____

_____

_____

_____

_____

_____

_____

_____

b. What will you do with your mate to communicate your desires to choose yourself?

_____

_____

_____

_____

_____

_____

_____

_____

_____

_____

c. What will you do this week to physically embrace and rejuvenate your spirit?

_____

_____

_____

_____

_____

_____

_____

_____

_____

_____

_____

d. What will you do to create a routine that chooses yourself and helps you maintain a personal sense of balance (e.g., make standing appointments to engage in a hobby, develop a friends' night out, exercise, etc.)?

_____

_____

_____

_____

_____

_____

_____

_____

_____

_____

_____

e. Knowing that change does not occur overnight, what will you do to negotiate and strike a compromise with your partner to assert your needs?

_____

_____

_____

_____

_____

_____

_____

_____

_____

_____

_____

f. What will you do to deal with the resistance and discomfort on the part of others (friends, children, family, etc.) as it relates to choosing yourself?

_____

_____

_____

_____

_____

_____

_____

_____

_____

_____

_____

THE CONQUERING

Little girl they say
You'll grow up to be a woman one day

Little girl they say
Prosperity and love will surely come your way

Grow up one day?
Don't these eyes tell
Though they are young, they've already seen hell!

Little girl they say
Save yourself for your wedding day

Wedding day?
I guess this means married at age five
Guests in attendance:
Confusion, betrayal, and fear though denied

Little girl they say
Take wings and fly
Clipped so young it hurts when I try

Little girl they say
Your beauty, can't you see?

Not with this captivity

Thoughts of love
Not for me
Not worth pennies beneath the sea
Perversion
Disgrace
In my mind no retreat

Little girl they say
Conquer and win
The secrecy, the shame, like shackles—the pain

Then with grace
You brought quiet and said
I Am The Divine
I Love You
You're Mine
Search from within
And then you will find
The end of your tears and clarity in time

Enlighten your mind
Then you will see
The strength you've been given
The choice to be free

I'll be your emblem
Take after me
An emblem of love
Love running free
Love that can heal the scars that you see

Be
Just be
The song of hope that I've created

Be
Just be
The voice no one can take from thee

Chapter 5
It's Time to Take Dominion

*I*n many cultures, the word *dominion* is defined as the power to direct, control, use, and dispose of. Simply, it refers to the principle of authority. The word *dominion* in conjunction with the phrase *moment of impact* can be quite meaningful to us when considering the terms in relation to each other. In general, a moment of impact is often defined as an action or event that makes an impression due to its timing, context, or delivery. One example of a moment of impact might be a new CEO announcing the adoption of an open-door policy and an internal collaborative approach to business at a historically cut-throat and internally competitive company while onlookers simultaneously witness each executive's office door being unhinged and removed by the company's maintenance crew. In this incident, the doors being unscrewed from their frames and removed from the building in conjunction with the announcement of a new work environment would be considered a moment of impact. Its timing, delivery, and context automatically affected those who witnessed the event. With deliberate and strategic intent, the CEO sought to gain everyone's attention by introducing information in a manner few would forget.

For obvious reasons, this impersonal event is not as emotionally laden as a personal one. However, personal ones are often more extreme. They have no middle ground—they are either perceived to be very positive or very negative. For example, the day a woman is proposed to by the one she loves represents a positive moment of impact, whereas the day a loved one is found dead at the scene of a crime represents a negative one. When positive, they serve to boost our esteem and create a sense of contentment. When negative, they can be traumatic, debilitating, and haunting. Additionally, they can emotionally victimize over and over, thus sustaining their effect for long periods. For some, these events become frozen situations unaffected by time and place. In this context, time may not promote a significant diminishing effect. Instead, it may provoke a mastery of avoidance, suppression, and denial. Whether a five-year-old girl or a woman of fifty, the power of these events to re-victimize or bring forth feelings of inadequacy, unhappiness, and fear remain relative. For this reason, people often become prisoners to their own moments of personal impact. As a prisoner, one is often controlled by the event in some way. This state of imprisonment can only be fought through the decision to move toward dominion and authority. The primary defense against permanent emotional scarring and prolonged devastation is the quest for dominion. In its essence, it requires a willingness to acknowledge our feelings (e.g., vulnerability, betrayal, violation) so we can take authority over the effects.

As a personal survivor of abuse, I know that the trip to authority over these experiences is not on the "best place to vacation" list. In my quest for dominion, I had to acknowledge my feelings of helplessness, betrayal, and anger just to begin my journey of putting the experience into perspective.

The process of trying to take authority over an event that happened more than twenty years ago was the hardest I had ever experienced. Recognizing that I still felt pain over the situation made me feel even more weak and vulnerable. As I made the conscious decision to move beyond faking that everything in my life was great, I had to stop avoiding certain conversations, feelings, childhood memories, and people. In other words, I was tired of being and feeling terrorized. I was also tired of terrorizing myself. Every time I hid from my emotional wounds and denounced my need for healing, I made the incidents more powerful than myself. For me, it took more than ten years to recognize my need for dominion and two years to achieve it. The quest for dominion is never an overnight process. Therefore, it especially interests me when I hear women say things like, "it happened and I'm over it," with *it* being the negative moment of impact. My consistent reaction of disbelief comes from the notion that you don't just get over it. Hence, I find the purpose of this statement to be one of convincing ourselves rather than the people to whom we proclaim it. In fact, I don't know that one ever "gets over" certain moments of impact. You can render it powerless over your emotions, behaviors, and decisions, but you don't just delete and forget it.

Many have tried to ignore these moments but the more you try to ignore them, the more they have a way of residing in your subconscious and manifesting in your behavior. For example, when I was a junior in college, I befriended a young man who confided in me about his girlfriend's struggle with insecurity. As our friendship grew, she, too, became an acquaintance, and I quickly noticed the behavior to which he often referred. Despite the challenge of her insecurity, they remained a couple. Then without warning or explanation, approximately one week prior to his graduation, she broke off the relationship.

My senior year, I reconnected with this young lady. One night we decided to go out to eat, and I tried to get her opinion on a problem I experienced with my parents earlier that evening. As we talked, it occurred to me that she only spoke of her mother, never her father. As I probed a bit, she remarked in a very flip and passive tone, "When I was seven, my so-called father said he was going to the store and I never saw him again; yeah, a trip ain't it, but I'm over it now." In that moment, it occurred to me she had yet to take dominion over her father's decision and the feelings it left behind. After years of friendship and lots of courageous therapeutic work on her part, she was able to admit that her college breakup was a classic case of her abandoning him before she could be left again. Through a great deal of introspection, she shared that her boyfriend's choice to attend graduate school took her back to being a devastated seven-year-old. For her, lack of dominion promoted denial and avoidance, which manifested itself as a fear of experiencing the same loss in most of her adult life. In an attempt to protect herself, she consistently severed commitments that heightened her subconscious fear of being deserted.

For many of us, negative moments of impact become life-altering events long after they happen. In an attempt to achieve emotional survival, many of our protective mechanisms attempt to save the day. As I see it, it's not the moment alone that poses the biggest problem, but the feelings of anger, powerlessness, and helplessness that abound as a result of it. Though none of us have control over the fact that bad things can and do happen, we do have power over how long we allow moments to affect our present and future circumstances. As women, our personal power is not just effective toward others, it works for us too. None of us can afford to harbor a spirit that is wounded. As a force of habit, we tend to view the concept of time as an ultimate healer. Although time is said to heal wounds, the assumption that it is the only needed remedy is a false one. It may help to diminish the visibility of your scars, but will not serve to totally cure the injury. In addition to time, the quest for dominion requires acknowledgement, forgiveness, and sometimes, disclosure. In many situations, it even demands the help of a third party (e.g., a therapist) to help support the process.

For many of us, acknowledgement is the hardest step because it totally confronts our mechanisms of avoidance. It will require you to exhibit a high level of honesty with yourself and others. It demands you accept that consistent denial, avoidance, and defensiveness does not work toward taking ownership of the incident and its influence on your life. Through acknowledgment you must confront the situation or circumstance and dissect the feelings attributed to the event(s). As you allow yourself to recognize your pain, you can expect to experience discomfort, vulnerability, and hesitation for emotions that may have never been truly realized or addressed before. This first step toward dominion sets the stage for breaking through burdensome feelings and achieving a greater sense of control. However, make no mistake, when you've been masking your pain for a long time, this can be a scary process.

Once you acknowledge the event, you must allow yourself time to fully experience your emotions. You have to embrace how you felt and how you feel. This step requires a great deal of support so don't shy away from seeking professional help to get you through. Dealing with your feelings is necessary because you can't achieve inner fulfillment if you are stuck in a negative space. To move out of this emotionally unproductive position, you must first forgive yourself for any unnecessary shame, guilt, and blame you may be carrying. In other words, take responsibility for the actions, decisions, and choices that belong to you and be compassionate, understanding and willing to stop relentlessly beating up on yourself. Remember, your spirit cannot thrive with you continuously kicking yourself. And, no matter the circumstance, you will always be worth forgiving and loving.

Once you've addressed personal feelings toward yourself, those for others will also need your attention. Though circumstances and situations may differ, forgiving others is a vital part of the dominion process. Without fail, it is one of the best healers of the spirit and providers of a true sense of freedom. When we don't forgive, we create a cyclical sense of personal terrorism by fueling the negativity of the person and incident while giving them power over our disposition, decisions, and emotions. As previously mentioned, no matter how it may seem, forgiveness is not a stamp of approval or release of responsibility. This couldn't be further from the truth. In fact, it de-emphasizes the power of those who hurt you while motivating your spirit to be empowered, try again, and control the only thing you can—yourself. It requires that you let go. It also forces you to assess how you truly feel about being pain free. Why? Over time, negative feelings may seem like permanent aspects of who we are, so getting rid of them may appear to be a loss in and of itself. It asks that we love ourselves enough to release anything that threatens our ability to love and feel loved, that we hold love as the standard despite wrongdoing. Forgiveness takes our moments of despair and offers the option of making those moments short lived. It is the foundation on which resolution stands firm. In its essence, it promotes a future free and unrepresentative of the past. With it, a foundation for personal resolution is promoted and the possibilities for positive human interaction are endless. Without it, the human spirit struggles for peace and experiences varying levels of self-destruction.

Last but not least, within the quest for dominion, is the issue of disclosure (breaking the silence). In our attempt to hide, avoid, and deny moments that caused pain, anger, and shame, we can submerge ourselves in bubbles of secrecy that often serve to create and perpetuate cycles of negativity and personal captivity. In many scenarios, disclosure is a necessary step toward closure and authority. Is it always required? No. However, despite the discomfort it may cause others, you own the right to tell your stories. You have the right to talk through your experiences. No, disclosure is not always necessary, but this assessment should not be attached to fear of people's responses and reactions. Instead, it should be attached to the lack of relevance and insignificance perceived by you.

The quest for dominion is hard for all of us, but choosing ourselves mandates it. You can free you. You deserve to be free of the fear and prolonged hurt that moments of impact often impart. No moment is worth conquering your laughter, joy, and future happiness. The effort is worth it, and so are you!

Insight
CORNER

1. *Define at least three significant moments of impact that represent painful experiences in your life.*

2. Do you feel like you have dominion over these experiences? If so, are there any other moments of impact that need to be considered?

a. *For the moments of impact that are still in need of dominion, how did these experiences make you feel?*

b. Acknowledge why these experiences were painful for you.

c. *What did you do to put an immediate bandage on the wounds that resulted from these moments?*

3. What do you perceive forgiveness would mean in each of these situations?

a. If you are or have beaten up on yourself for a moment of impact, how could you start to move toward self-forgiveness?

b. *As it relates to others, how can you move toward forgiving those involved in your defined moments of impact? What steps will you take to move toward forgiveness?*

4. If you have tried to forgive and your moment(s) of impact continue to have lingering effects on your life, what will you do to reach out and seek professional help? What is your timeline to start this process?

...To There

*L*ife is a gift. Living is a choice. We can either dwell in obstacles and be shackled by our past or see the possibilities, embrace the unknown, and acknowledge that life is worth living to the fullest. Life is a gift. Living is a choice. It's your time. Move to there and journey toward a more fruitful future.

WITH PURPOSE

One's reflection
So interesting a thing

Is it one dimensional?

Couldn't be

Look a little closer
There is so much there to see

One dimensional?
Not if you look closely
So many layers intricately

The first most obviously
The ones behind create a true vision of complexity
Layers of faith, resilience, ambition, and insight
Layers of knowledge, courage, and love

All encompassed if you are willing to see
A vision of passion, purpose, and desires to be

The goal?
The goal is forever twofold
To appreciate and know

Appreciate your reflection
Its entirety is magnificent

Appreciate passion
It clarifies purpose

Appreciate worth
You define your value

Know that your presence
Does make a difference

Know that you are
Your strongest ally

One dimensional?
Couldn't be

Look a little closer
Look until you see
The brilliance of your reflection

Your true reality!

Chapter 6
And Then There Was Vision!

ost men would agree that women are some of the greatest consumers of products and services. More bluntly, men often accuse our entire gender of being never-ending shopaholics. As women, we spend billions of dollars a year. Most of us purchase by preference, affordability, and necessity. However, we rarely think of the companies that create the products we buy. Few of us consider the corporate vision of the businesses we patronize. Though vision may not be at the forefront of our minds as consumers, its importance is unwavering. In fact, it is so important to the development of what we spend our money on, few would argue that the success and profitability of a business are dependent on it. Though a company's vision may change as time, capabilities, and markets evolve, it is ever present. By all accounts, the who, when, where, and how of the business world usually comes from the courage to envision and articulate the vision (e.g., the what).

As it relates to us as women, vision is as critical to business as it is to our personal success. It is the picture created in your mind that embraces possibility, desire, and courage while denouncing feasibility, fears, and foes. As we journey beyond baggage toward fulfillment the word *purpose* will be at many crossroads along the way. As we travel we will inevitably run across the following questions: What am I doing? What do I want to do? Is this what I was meant to do? All of these questions surround one's personal calling. I use the word *calling* because everyone has one, a reason for which one's life was given. I would even go as far as to say the seeds (talents and passions) of purpose are given with the gift of life. Now, how do purpose and vision fit? Purpose is defined through listening to the internal desires that relate to talent and passion. However, it is often realized and achieved through the creation of a vision that motivates movement and exploration, thus leading to discovery of what needs to be done to accomplish one's goals.

To many of us, the term *purpose* can be quite exhausting and overwhelming. If you don't believe me, the next time you meet with some of your girlfriends, ask them what they believe is their life's purpose. Once the question has been posed, be ready to witness looks of intense thought followed by a bunch of incomplete sentences, alluding to the fact that you have just sent their minds into complete overdrive.

Without fail, this question usually creates a sense of despair, anxiety, and confusion or a sense of happiness, excitement, and peace. Why? Because the life's purpose question usually triggers other thoughts like: Where am I going with my life? Am I truly happy? Should I be doing something else? Am I doing what I was put on Earth to do?

For obvious reasons, the complexity of these questions forces us to feel discomfort with the mundane, monotonous, and minuscule aspects of life. However, these questions are critical because they make it hard for us to continuously ignore our passions, talents, and uniqueness. It forces us to look beyond the conventional cookbook approach (e.g., go to school to get a job that financially supports you) toward that of the individual masterpiece approach (e.g., identify your passion, cultivate it, and get people to pay you for doing it). Though many of us have felt obligated to the cookbook approach, the latter is more applicable to finding and living within purpose and realizing one's true potential. Indeed, both roads are fulfilling in their own right, but living within one's purpose is more rewarding, gratifying, and satisfying.

In general, conversations about purpose are very thought-provoking. For the most part, four things usually happen when the questions surrounding purpose arise: 1) we choose not to entertain them and pretend they don't exist; 2) we contemplate the questions and get stuck on how to move forward; 3) we become saddened by the fact that we haven't moved toward our known purpose, and, therefore, immobilize ourselves from ever moving forward; or 4) we contemplate the questions and with or without knowing how, we decide to embark on the journey of discovery.

From a personal perspective, I have contemplated the question of purpose too many times to count. I finally decided to stop bumping my head against the question and made the scary decision to try and move toward finding the answer. Like many of you, I recognized very early in my adulthood that life could be okay if I just decided to do the basics: get a job and acquire a few material things (e.g., car, apartment, furniture, and clothes). In fact, no one would be upset or disappointed in me—no one except me. If this were my decision, I would not have been alone. Many people have settled for less than living within their personal purpose because they have convinced themselves that it is nonexistent, too hard to attain, or too late to achieve. Some have swallowed the myth that purpose is a once-in-a-lifetime opportunity that they missed and others have become experts at why they can't embrace their purpose rather than why they can.

If you wonder whether or not you are one of these people, assess how many times a month you feel like you're not exactly doing what you love or what you want to do. If you don't have many fingers left, you may be misusing your energy for little return. It matters not your age and circumstance; what matters is how much you are willing to think outside of the box to embrace the journey of purpose. For example, if you are a thirty-eight-year-old who has always wanted to help heal the sick through medicine, have you engaged in a process that will move you toward this destination? Hmmm! If at the age of thirty-eight you are struggling with why this desire is not realistic at this point in your life, consider the fact that you probably had this same yearning at ages twenty, twenty-three, twenty-eight, thirty, and thirty-four. Despite the car, house, promotions, designer shoes, mate, kids, and financial investments, this voice still won't shut up! Well, it's time to recognize that this void won't just disappear. Look forward to seeing it again at forty-three, fifty, and fifty-five unless you do something about it. The reason is simple: Avoidance is not a true escape! In fact, actions that do not surround purpose tend to keep you yearning for it.

You can almost guarantee your heart will always remind you that you are not doing what you should. The more you try to ignore your purpose, the more it will refuse to be ignored. The more you try to silence the desires within, the more you will see that no accomplishment can compare to its fulfillment. Knowing this reality, it didn't take long for me to figure out I couldn't deal with this type of torture. I had to be authentic with myself. I couldn't pretend my heart's desires didn't exist. I couldn't embrace a lifetime of wishing and never trying. So, I could either fight against my gifts or attempt to find creative ways to align my activities with what I thought was my reason for being, my purpose.

As a woman, it doesn't take much to see that we are all splendidly different. Our diverse talents and desires make us all unique. Again, these items serve as messengers. If you listen—devoid of fear, circumstance, or doubt—you will discover that together, talents and passions provide hints about what you should be doing with your life. In their most infantile state, they serve as fundamental parts of a personal vision. These elements exist whether we want to admit it or not.

A friend of mine made a statement that needed to be challenged: "What if you don't have any gifts and nothing stimulates you, what do you do if you are that person?" I answered by saying, "You keep thinking, searching, and listening." I further went on to explain that acknowledging and achieving purpose is easier for some than others.

She then said, "What if you don't like to do anything in particular, for example, what if the only thing you like to do is eat, what's the purpose in that?" To her surprise I then said, "Eating is a legitimate passion." Then I challenged her to think about how eating could be turned into a lucrative and fulfilling lifestyle. I suggested that eating was the profession of most food critics, food testers, dieticians, chefs, food journalists, food photographers, nutritionists, and the like, so the question was not about purpose. As I explained to her, the issue was more about embracing eating as a passion and looking beyond convention to find creative ways of experiencing and living within that passion every single day.

Like this example, most of us can identify a minimal sense of what we feel passionate about, what our talents are, and what we desire. However, we are often socialized to suppress, deny, and belittle these aspects of ourselves rather than explore, cultivate, and pursue them. As a result, we often speak of these elements in the past tense: I wanted to, I wish I had, if I only knew, if I could, and so on. Well, I know one thing for sure, if you are reading this book, it's definitely not too late to create a purpose-led vision for yourself. If you've given up on your vision, it's never too late to remotivate yourself and try again. The only thing in this lifetime that can stop the fulfillment of purpose is death. Children, marriage, responsibilities, obligation, and age should not be used as excuses to give up on yourself.

A while back, a young lady told me that she couldn't just decide to go to law school because she had children to support. After revealing how unhappy she was, I asked her if she was willing to make small steps toward purpose rather than more steps toward further unhappiness. Eliminating one "I couldn't" and "I can't" after another, she started to embrace the idea that she could make the decision to seek employment in a law firm, gain some experience, and with a little ingenuity, get her employer to pay for her to attend law school. There was a way to be a good mom and choose herself at the same time. Though it wouldn't be an easy nor overnight transition, it was possible and plausible. Recognizing that no one was benefiting from her stress and unhappiness, not even her children, she disclosed that fear was debilitating her. As a result, she stopped believing in the likelihood of becoming a lawyer and gave up on the possibility of living within her purpose. She, too, had to admit that the only thing that stops you from realizing and living within your purpose is you. As we ended our conversation, she embraced the reality that she had choices. So, I will say to you like I said to her, "It's time to get up and move out of your own way!"

For each of us, the choice to listen to our desires, create a personal vision, investigate available resources, make a plan, follow it, give our best effort, and embrace the journey of discovery is one only we can make. I truly believe death and personal choice are the only things that keep us from purpose. Stop letting the nouns (people, places, or things) cheat you out of what you were put here to do. We can no longer stand on the sidelines of our own lives. We must formulate a vision and move toward fulfilling it. As we travel, the vision may change, however, we must continue to strive knowing that we will gain invaluable insight that will lead to our appropriate destinations.

If by chance you are experiencing a struggle like the woman with the passion for eating, you do have a purpose. When you think out loud, there are desires that continue to resurface. When you don't allow yourself to think about why it can't happen, why it's a stupid thought, why it's not the best time to try, or why the obstacles are too big, what do you come up with? For me, there is no question in my mind that my life's purpose was revealed in this manner. When I thought of what made me happiest, I had to take an honest inventory of my God-given gifts and talents and dare to stop doubting myself. I recognized that I had a gift of song and seemed happiest when I felt like I was helping to empower women. Though I wasn't clear about how these two talents would come together, I started finding ways to cultivate them separately (e.g., joined a musical theater guild and became a peer educator for young girls). With no recipe for success besides some good old-fashioned hard work, I began to seek opportunities that would allow me to do the things I loved to do the most. The more I did so, the more I started figuring out how they defined my purpose.

As I embraced my talents, I was able to start creating a vision (the what), but I still needed to figure out the how, when, and where. Interestingly enough, the how is an ever-changing answer. When I began my journey, I prayed that the necessary tools to solidify my vision would be revealed to me because at first I was a bit unsure of where to begin. I couldn't figure out how to reach out to women in a manner that would make them receptive to what I had to offer. Once this question was on the table, it was hard to ignore I had what my friends called the gift of gab. Time and time again, I was told I had an uncanny ability to talk to people and be heard. Yet, the thought of using my skill to communicate as a tool to achieve purpose was a bit of a stretch for me. The more I contemplated the concept, the more I toiled over where I could find captive and receptive audiences. The answer was not cut and dry. From the standpoint of feasibility, I was not famous, full of elderly wisdom, nor a psychologist or motivational speaker at the time. Who would want to listen to me? I almost talked myself out of trying to continue on the path, but, when I stopped embracing doubt, I started to seek opportunities.

After much deliberation, I decided to explore some of the organizations that were said to focus on the needs of women in my community. At the time, I became a volunteer at a battered women's shelter. When I started, I volunteered on the crisis hot line talking to one woman at a time. By the time I left the shelter, I was a support-group leader talking to groups of women all the time. My work with them led to opportunities in other organizations and the domino effect toward my vision started to take effect. Those experiences became building blocks that helped to clarify the specifics of my purpose: to empower women through words, speaking, and song.

With this, I pose the question, what do you have to lose? Your ability to envision the possibilities for your life is a major contributor to your success. It is your responsibility to claim what is rightfully yours, the opportunity to achieve greatness. You have to recognize how strong and dynamic you are. For what do you want to be remembered? What would be the absolute worst thing that could happen if you took a chance on yourself and tried to make it happen? When you saw the cover of this book, you saw my name and decided I was an author. I became an author the day I expanded my personal vision and decided that I could. I envisioned the book's completion and without a sense of knowing, I began to write. With an empty computer screen and pages unwritten, I chose to embrace the journey. The fact that you are reading this book is a testament to the truth in a popular saying: In order to be something you've never been, you must be willing to do something you've never done. How much longer will you wait? See it! Believe it! Do it!

Insight
CORNER

1. Do you feel you are presently moving within your personal purpose? If not, why?

2. Do you have a sense of what your personal purpose is? If so, what is it?

3. If you are not clear on your purpose, answer the following questions to start moving toward discovery.

a. What stimulates you? More specifically, what are you passionate about?

b. *What do you consider to be your natural talents?*

c. What do you really enjoy doing?

d. *Are there things you never have an opportunity to do that comes to mind over and over?*

4. *Have you chosen to explore any of your passions, gifts, or talents as a career or a major portion of your livelihood? If not, why?*

a. *If you could turn your talent/passion into a career or a major part of your livelihood, what would it be?*

5. *What issues, people, or circumstances debilitate your efforts or discourage your exploration process?*

6. *Pushing fear aside, create your personal vision statement. For example, my personal vision is to use my public speaking, writing, and lyrical ability as a tool to inspire and motivate women in their personal journey toward empowerment, fulfillment, and purpose.*

7. *List five short-term, intermediate, and long-term goals to help you move from where you are to living out your vision statement.*

8. What actions will be needed to fulfill your short-term goals (e.g., what, when, where, and how)?

_____

_____

_____

_____

_____

_____

_____

_____

_____

_____

_____

_____

_____

_____

_____

_____

_____

_____

_____

_____

_____

_____

_____

_____

_____

a. What resources will you need to help you achieve your short-term goals (e.g., who and what)?

b. What is your timeline for accomplishing your short-term goals (e.g., start date/
   completion date)?

_____

_____

_____

_____

_____

_____

_____

_____

_____

_____

_____

_____

_____

_____

_____

_____

_____

_____

_____

_____

_____

_____

_____

_____

_____

c. How will you know when your short-term goals have been met/achieved?

9. *What actions will be needed to fulfill your intermediate goals (e.g., what, when, where, and how)?*

a. What resources will you need to help you achieve your intermediate goals (e.g., who and what)?

b. What is your timeline for accompoishing your intermediate goals (e.g., start date/
   completion date)?

c. How will you know when your intermediate goals have been met?

10. *What actions will be needed to fulfill your long-term goals (e.g., what, when, where, and how)?*

_____

_____

_____

_____

_____

_____

_____

_____

_____

_____

_____

_____

_____

_____

_____

_____

_____

_____

_____

_____

_____

_____

_____

_____

_____

_____

Nicole LaBeach

a. What resources will you need to help you achieve your long-term goals (e.g., who and what)?

b. What is your timeline for accomplishing your long-term goals (e.g., start date/
  completion date)?

_____

_____

_____

_____

_____

_____

_____

_____

_____

_____

_____

_____

_____

_____

_____

_____

_____

_____

_____

_____

_____

_____

_____

_____

_____

c. How you will know when your long-term goals have been met/achieved?

11. Identify and contact one to two people with whom you can share your plan. Ask them to partner with you and help to keep you accountable to your goals, plans, and personal timeline.

Person 1: ————————————————————————————

Goal date to contact them: ————————————————————————

Person 2: ————————————————————————————

Goal date to contact them: ————————————————————————

STONE WALLS

So you need a breakthrough
Something just to help you believe in you
Lingering and doubtful
Don't give up
Don't give in
You've come through worse
Remember…

You are where you are
But you're not where you're going
So
Know
And be convinced in your knowing
That you can
You can move through

You will
You will move through
Move with a force of self-determination
Move with the fearlessness of an eagle

Just when you think you have no strength left
Spirit weary
Body worn
Take a look
Look behind you
Check out the scene
The trail of stones evidence the truth
The wall that you broke through the last time
Remember?
Once again
Another victory is in sight
So keep on moving
Dare to keep moving
And just when it seems like the road is endless

Remember
Never forget
Every testimony
Starts with a TEST!

Chapter 7
Beyond the Bumps

*H*appiness versus sadness, good versus evil, every cloud has a silver lining—all of these examples represent the law of opposites. This law suggests everything has two sides. To many, these phrases define and categorize how we look at occurrences in our everyday lives. They help us recognize actions, circumstances, and situations as positive or negative. Positive sides of the law are often seen as blessings and good fortune. For obvious reasons, the negative sides are perceived as obstacles and misfortune. The negative sides, or what I consider to be the adversarial bumps of life present a clear challenge. Though it may be presumptive on my part, I assume none of us are strangers to the term adversity (e.g., hard times, uphill battles, etc.). In fact, many of us know adversity on a first-name basis.

Whether met in the form of injustice, a lack of resources, unfortunate circumstances, or the like, many of us know the term and its implications better than we like to admit. As metaphoric heroes, we all have boxes of memorabilia that represent our battles with ups and downs. Some of the items symbolize victories and others surrender, but all show varying levels of casualty and survival. Unfortunately, the artifacts that speak of our fortitude and natural ability to overcome obstacles are often overshadowed and forgotten. When it relates to the achievement of purpose, fulfillment, and wholeness, our power is often overlooked. Not by others, but by us. When required to use the same stamina with which we fight for others, for personal use, we doubt and de-emphasize our own abilities. This may be due to the fact that many of us build our combat strength on situations and events that do not concern our personal evolvement. Therefore, when we have to fight for ourselves it can seem like frightening and unfamiliar territory. This feeling diminishes our perceived connection between former victories and current odds, which in turn promotes the desire to retreat.

In general, the battlefield en route to fulfilling purpose is unlike others. It's different for the main reason that the battle toward purpose is all about you. As we venture to choose ourselves, we must seek to embrace, understand, and achieve that for which we were given life. In doing so, we can all expect to endure a challenge or three along the way. With adversity being the opposite side of prosperity, its attendance in the journey toward purpose is inevitable. In this vein, its main goal is to deter, confuse, or change one's course toward purpose. It seeks to distort personal vision, promote fear, and diminish your ability to believe in your goals and yourself. Like the unknown, adversity is to be expected. However, when it strikes, use your weapons of faith, persistence, and confidence to overcome it.

Though we're often expected to be independent, few of us have been encouraged to settle for nothing less than embracing and discovering our purpose. In fact, if our passion and potential had no conventional career path, it was often belittled or disregarded. For the most part, our dreams, talents, and passions were often turned into hobbies because we were told they couldn't be turned into a main portion of our livelihood. Hence, the lessons that taught happiness as something disjointed from purpose began. In an attempt to make us practical, many of us were encouraged to move away from our gifts and talents rather than within them. Hence, purpose was rarely promoted much less embraced as a vehicle to move us toward a true sense of fulfillment. As a result, the achievement of it was viewed as an unrealistic option. However, the truth of the matter is, unveiling, embracing, and living within one's purpose is one of the most rewarding and realistic goals for which to strive.

As we seek to live a life that celebrates choosing ourselves, we must recognize the importance of purpose and how it is often intertwined with adversarial situations or the bumps and bruises of life. In a nutshell, if adversity is a guaranteed aspect of living and breathing, it seems logical to experience them as they connect to our most fulfilling destination—purpose. Unfortunately, some of us have accepted the fallacy that purpose is too hard to attempt. True enough, living in one's purpose takes work and commitment, but what doesn't? If adversity is not enough to make you quit when it comes to other journeys and circumstances within your life, why should it be acceptable when it comes to your own purpose? Don't look at it as the fight of your life, look at it as the fight *for* your life! It's time to recognize life's trials and tribulations are not a permission slip to give up. Nor do they justify finding other time-consuming options that deter you from what you ought to be doing and where you ought to be going.

At any given point in your life, you are either entering a storm, in the midst of a storm, or moving out of a storm. With each move, your objective should be to press forward as the wind and rain try to push you backward. If you don't allow yourself to be consumed with fear of the unknown, you can look through the intensity of the wind knowing the pressure will eventually decrease and the yardage covered will increase as a result of your efforts. Remember, the other side of adversity is prosperity. But the question is, are you ready to stop looking at the bumps as defining moments and look at them as a mere means to an end? In life, there is no such thing as an indefinite setback or failure because every lesson learned up to that point can be used to maximize your efforts when you try again. It's up to you to look beyond the walls that appear to be made of stone and kick them down. Choose yourself. Stretch forward and go for it. You and everyone around you will have much to gain from your courage to embrace what you deserve.

Insight
CORNER

1. *As it relates to your journey toward personal purpose, what obstacles and bouts with adversity have deterred your efforts?*

2. How can you use previous victories and triumphs as tools of motivation in your journey toward purpose?

Nicole LaBeach

3. What kind of support system can you create to encourage you when you feel like giving up?

4. What action(s) will you take to put this support system in place?

THE DESTINATION

This day is the happiest there could ever be
Or is it?

Back there
Many accomplishments by me
Moments of triumph
Worthy to see

Looking back it's strange to see
Strange that there's little reverence from me

Race to the finish line
So many moments cut short

Moments unacknowledged
Moments gone too soon

How much did I miss?
Miss by the question too quickly asked
What next?

Chapter 8
Your Presence Is Requested

*A*s women, we have grown into our adulthood with the help of other women. For some of us, they inspired us to do well, achieve great things, and be the best we could ever hope to be. These women motivated our personal ambitions and gave us the model of superwomanhood. For me, many of these women prided themselves on doing twenty hours of work in fifteen and passed on the same value system to me. Their model taught me how to be a driven multitasking machine. I remember looking back and wondering when I caught the superwoman bug. Though I couldn't precisely pinpoint when it started, I remember moving toward the status of being a well-oiled machine living on fumes at age eighteen. Unlike an automobile, I required little gas and minimal maintenance to keep going. I had goals, direction, and many things needed to be done to get me to the "theres" of my life. I started on a superwoman path without even knowing it. My motto—I can do it, and do it I did!

Now, a tad bit older and wiser, I see things differently. Though I still celebrate ambition and a strong work ethic, I recognize all women are in danger of a fundamental problem: tunnel vision. When we move with tunnel vision toward our personal destinations, the beauty of the journey often becomes invisible. As we take on more responsibility, higher expectations, and varying definitions of success, the proverbial race begins. As a result, we continue to miss the natural sites along the way that warrant a moment of attention. We forget that part of choosing ourselves includes taking the time to revere the gift of every day and all that happens within it.

Being part of a generation who has made more money and experienced more opportunities than the previous, many of us have felt great pressure to reach our goals and the various finish lines we create for ourselves. This cycle of racing to complete one goal after another perpetuates a lack of presence that makes some of life's most valuable moments nothing more than a blur. I learned this lesson the hard way. As you look at the cover of this book, you'll see the book title, my name, and three little letters (Ph.D.). It still pains me to admit that I missed most of the doctoral journey. Like many other things in my life, I wanted it, pursued it, and achieved it. During this process, I focused on the challenges in front of me and tried to always stay one step ahead of the game. I was always sure to juggle more than one goal at a time, and as I accomplished them, I just kept on moving. Rarely did I come up for air and take into account the obstacles I successfully overcame. In doing so, the essence of the experience passed me by and made for an anticlimactic ending. Like other challenges, once the race began, completing the goal quickly became the destination. However, the challenges within the journey and my determination often worked together to render me emotionally absent from many of the successes along the way. As a result, achievements that should have been eventful, like receiving my master's degree, were just a matter of process.

For me, finishing my master's degree just promoted the question, "How much further to the doctorate?" I got so caught up in the destination that I missed some of the best parts of the journey. Like many women, I missed the part where you say to yourself "great job;" the part where you take a moment to look at how strikingly fabulous you really are as a woman; the moment where you choose yourself by recognizing, applauding, and rewarding your own effort. In my eagerness to arrive at the destination, my appreciation for the process and myself was often rushed or worse yet, overlooked. The experience of acquiring a Ph.D. taught me many things. For starters, the physical aspects of any journey are an inevitable requirement (e.g., studying, gaining practical experience, taking exams, etc.), however, the recognition of personal triumphs and successes are choices that should never be surpassed. Though the destination is important, the journey is also critical. Even in times of turmoil, it offers gifts of joy to behold, but the decision to embrace, devalue, or ignore them on the way to the next challenge is a personal one. Now, I can admit getting lost in a goal or taking life way too seriously is still a daily struggle for me, however, I am up for the challenge, and I know I am not alone in this fight.

As we move from one accomplishment to another we must recognize our presence is necessary. Personal fulfillment requires that we stop to smell the flowers in our lives. All parts of the journey (the beginning, middle, and end) require your presence, not just the ultimate destinations. Although many of us feel like it's a fight to justify consistent presence in our hectic lifestyles, we must remember time will keep ticking whether or not we take a moment to observe our surroundings, laugh, rejuvenate, or depressurize.

As women, our presence validates that we are indeed embracing life in its entirety. It reminds us to be the first to acknowledge ourselves. It encourages us to validate our own achievements and reminds us that we are indeed the best note takers of our own personal journey. With an inability to read into the future, it's impossible to know which experiences are most valuable and most important. Therefore, we must choose to acknowledge every moment we can. For all of us, life lessons are determined by the journey. To miss it would mean missing the insight and "ahhh-hahs" that often make for the sweetest memories and quite frankly, some of the most heartfelt laughter.

So, if you are presently reading this and saying to yourself, *I'll get to it, I don't have time, I am way too busy,* STOP! Stop and ask yourself why you are not choosing to fully engage in your own life. No matter the goal, obligation, responsibility, or expectation—ownership and recognition of your happiness is the foundation from which all other potential sources of fulfillment will flow. So dare to look around and receive all that deserves to be noticed. As you do so, you may find acknowledging "here" is the biggest part of what makes "there" so incredible.

1. *List at least five significantly positive things that have happened to you within the past five years.*

2. When these moments occurred, did you give yourself and the event(s) the recognition they deserved? If not, why not?

3. What are some things in your life that deserve to be noticed on a daily basis but rarely get your attention?

4. Do you ever shortchange yourself by minimizing your accomplishments or prematurely racing toward the next goal or challenge? Why do you think you do that?

5. What can you do to practice embracing the moment instead of instantly racing toward the next challenge?

6. *Racing through your life denounces the spirit of choosing yourself. Knowing this, how can you promote a continuous sense of reflection and rejuvenation in your schedule?*

a. *What can you do on a weekly basis to reaffirm your worth so you don't minimize how dynamic and valuable you truly are?*

SUNRISE

What if I
Stopped wishing that yesterday could be different
Stopped living for other people's expectations
Stopped working hard for things I didn't want
And stopped being so hard on myself

What if I
Stopped taking myself for granted
Stopped perpetuating the mundane
and challenged my thoughts
Stopped doing the same thing
and expecting a different result

What if I
Stopped wishing I could turn back time
Stopped giving so much and expecting so little
Stopped minimizing my dreams
and started moving toward them

What if I
Stopped doubting myself
And stopped belittling my strength

Would the world end?

What if I
Started to live
Started to make my own rules
Started to let go of the past
And started to embrace every day as a blessing

What if I
Started to do what made me happy
Started to make choices that celebrated my womanhood
And started to appreciate my unique beauty

What if I
Started to believe that I truly could

What if I
Started to celebrate all that is me
Started to give myself the best and expect nothing less
And started to let my faith paralyze my fears

What if I
Loved the woman I am unconditionally
Embraced my personal purpose daily
Laughed a little more
And cried a little less

Would the world end?
No

Living would begin!

Chapter 9
Today Is . . .

*L*ife is indeed funny. Maybe it's because the journey from there...to there is a never-ending cycle that presents every day as another chance to follow our heart, move beyond basic survival, and embrace personal peace. Every day is yet another opportunity to get you "there," and when you get "there," you will inevitably find another "there" to desire. Why? The "theres" of life represent metaphoric progressions.

Minute by minute the world as we know it changes like we do. As each day presents new challenges and a hopeful step closer to our goals, we are given the charge to embrace the ride and take good pictures of the view. If we're true to the process of personal discovery and jump in with both feet, there promises never to be a dull moment. We can look forward to a litany of questions, numerous quests for answers, and even expect an epiphany or two along the way. If we're lucky, the insight received will bring us closer to an appreciation for just how special the journey truly is. The voyage is there to promote growth, not a jaded sense of reality. Like a seed that's planted and breaks through the earth to blossom into its fullness, we, too, must break through to the endless possibilities that seek to move us from basic satisfaction to a higher sense of purpose, connectedness, and authenticity. Every day is a new day of commitment to being our best. Despite what did or didn't happen yesterday, today is a new beginning.

For me, February 15 will forever be special. This day brought forth an unexpected gift of hope for the present and the future. As I moved from one meeting to the next, I pondered what I would say. When, I called Mrs. McIntosh to announce that I would be late, I couldn't help but think of their faces. How did I want our time to be remembered? As I rushed up the stairs, I tried to stay calm; I walked down the hall, took a deep breath, and put my hand on the door to enter into the moment. There they were, a roomful of them. Their eyes piercing with curiosity, their excitement matching mine, I felt honored. I entered a bulletin board-filled classroom to experience the genuine enthusiasm of fifth-grade girls waiting feverishly for my arrival. They were my dream audience. So impressionable, so open, so optimistic…but what I had prepared to say seemed unbefitting. As I scrambled to rethink my presentation, we talked about their educational foundation, and I praised their potential. Like many others, I inquired about what they wanted to be when they grew up. They spoke of dreams to make you proud. Their innocence, bliss, and enthusiasm took me back twenty years. They had it. They had a pure and unadulterated sense of optimism. Collectively, they had a sense of fulfillment and happiness yet untarnished. They had big dreams, all of which they felt could be accomplished. As I listened to them, it occurred to me: they saw every day as a new day. For them, each morning was a new chance to dream, laugh, and love. This premise alone made their futures full of promise.

Well, I had dared to think it, so it had to be said, "Today is the first day of the rest of your life." Then it happened, I received an opportunity to see hope at its best, a roomful of potential, shouting this phrase at the top of their lungs, as if it were a powerful mantra. As they screamed "Today is the first day of the rest of my life" over and over, it occurred to me, I was the one who needed to hear it. Like many women, I was the one who needed to take ownership of it. As I listened, I wished that every day would reinforce this empowering belief. Through the growing pains, disappointments, and obstacles, I wished they would view each morning as a renewed first day to choose themselves. Every "today" would be a new opportunity to see how much practice made a difference, that dreams deserved to be explored, and their worth would forever be priceless. Every "today" would be embraced as one full of possibilities for forgiveness, overcoming adversity, and living within purpose. Every "today" would give them an opportunity to see things differently, leave yesterday behind, and embrace the sun.

What I wished for them, I, too, needed to consistently reaffirm within myself. On that day, I went to inspire, and I received inspiration. This phrase, which is often overused, seemed different. In its simplicity, it seemed like for the first time, I truly understood what it meant to declare "Today is the first day of the rest of my life." My fifth-grade spirit was renewed. In one visit, a group of girls reaffirmed everything I had spent months writing about. In that one day, they reinforced my belief that attitude is truly the first step toward happiness. In a very real sense, I could see in them the ability to be anything and go anywhere. Their belief in themselves would serve to navigate authority over their personal journey and help to determine their bumps, bruises, and bounce-backs along the way. Without knowing it, they were on a course that would take them places both frequently and less traveled. What their tomorrows would bring, no one would know, but how they received their challenges and resolved their baggage would establish their ability to take life by storm. They were examples to live for and live by. In them, I saw how powerful the phrase "Today is the first day of the rest of your life" really was. Simply, it offers a lifetime of chances despite moments of the past. It begs that you take a chance and choose yourself because you are truly the best thing that could have ever happened to you.

In one moment, a group of ten-year-olds and eleven-year-olds validated what my spirit had struggled with most of my adult life: that purpose, wholeness, and fulfillment were daily choices every woman has to make to live her life to the fullest. Every day presents another opportunity not to give up on being your best self. And, each dawn is filled with a new outlook. It's time, isn't it? It's time to seek what you want out of life, to heal, and to commit to your own sense of peace. As I remember their faces, I recognize their innocence had a flame of bravery and entitlement toward good that could only be dimmed by future experiences seeking to denounce their self-esteem. For them, fear would be the enemy and powerlessness their threatening illusion. However, the best we could ever give them as women is lessons on how to choose themselves through our own living and breathing example. For them and for all of us, self is where the journey toward fulfillment, purpose, and wholeness begins. So, what will you do with today? Will you choose to move? Will you choose to try? Will you choose to live? Will you choose?

Choose yourself...No one has ever been more worth it!

Insight
CORNER

1. *If today were the last day of your life, what would you have done with your life that you have yet to do?*

2. Are any of the items part of your personal vision? If not, why not? How can you implement some of these items into your personal vision and journey toward your purpose?

_____

_____

_____

_____

_____

_____

_____

_____

_____

_____

_____

_____

_____

_____

_____

_____

_____

_____

_____

_____

_____

_____

_____

_____

_____

_____

3. Viewing today as the first day of the rest of your life, what will you do to embrace the present and celebrate your future?

4. When you feel discouraged and experience adversity, what will you commit to doing to keep you striving for your dreams?

5. What will you do to always reaffirm that your presence and purpose are important?

6. *What will you do to choose yourself and make the most of every day from this moment forward?*

About the Author
& Volition Enterprises Inc.

Nicole LaBeach is the founder of Volition Enterprises, Inc. whose mission is to empower women through the provision of products, seminars, and key note addresses that offer motivational, inspirational, and strategic tools for living a balanced, purpose-driven and fulfilled life. Nicole received her Ph.D. in organizational psychology and her master's degree in research with a concentration in clinical psychology from St. Louis University in St. Louis, Missouri. Nicole's bachelor's degree in psychology was received from Spelman College in Atlanta, Georgia. Her professional career includes work with News Corporation (parent company of all FOX entities), Anheuser-Busch Corporation, and Provident Counseling.

As a public speaker, Nicole is an inspiration. Her compassion, honesty, and integrity captivate audiences while challenging them to overcome adversity and embrace personal possibilities. Her communication style has made her a compelling leader in the next generation of psychologists and life strategists, and a sought-after speaker to women in both professional and nonprofessional arenas. Nicole's dedication to the empowerment of women has a long track record that extends from research on attitudes toward rape victims and sexual harassment in the workplace to working with organizations on the advocacy of women. Nicole is a true example of what can happen if one embraces personal purpose and moves beyond life's misfortunes and adversities. Her dedication to strategic endeavors that alleviate the hardships and challenges of women is a purpose for which she was called.

To schedule Dr. Nicole LaBeach for a conference, workshop, or speaking engagement contact: yourvolition@aol.com

To order items from the Choose Yourself series (books, journals, organizers, stationary, and CD's) please visit
www.volitionenterprises.com